Praise

'Nic Marks has long championed the radical idea that happiness is a metric worth measuring. This book shows it's more than that – it's the secret sauce behind every thriving team.'
— Chris Anderson, Head of TED

'If we want a better future, we must build happier workplaces. *Happiness Is a Serious Business* offers the science – and the soul – to make it real.'
— Mo Gawdat, former Chief Business Officer at Google X and author of *Solve for Happy*

'Everyone wants greater positive performance and happiness at work. This book provides an evidence-based, practical way to accomplish that in the modern working world.'
— Shawn Achor, *New York Times* bestselling author of *The Happiness Advantage*

HAPPINESS IS A SERIOUS BUSINESS

Why happy teams are more successful and how to build them

Nic Marks

R^ethink

First published in Great Britain in 2025
by Rethink Press (www.rethinkpress.com)

© Copyright Nic Marks

All rights reserved. No part of this publication may be reproduced, stored in or introduced into a retrieval system, or transmitted, in any form, or by any means (electronic, mechanical, photocopying, recording or otherwise) without the prior written permission of the publisher.

The right of Nic Marks to be identified as the author of this work has been asserted by him in accordance with the Copyright, Designs and Patents Act 1988.

This book is sold subject to the condition that it shall not, by way of trade or otherwise, be lent, resold, hired out, or otherwise circulated without the publisher's prior consent in any form of binding or cover other than that in which it is published and without a similar condition including this condition being imposed on the subsequent purchaser.

Contents

Preface: From Numbers To People And
    Numbers About People   1

Introduction: Happiness Is A Serious Business   7

PART ONE   Understanding Happiness   15

1 The Inevitable (And Measurable) Ups
    And Downs Of Happiness   17

2 Happiness: More Than A Yellow Emoji   27

3 The Dynamics Of Happiness   35

4 Boredom Is A Joy Killer   41

5 A Lesson From Smokers   47

6 Happiness Is Deeply Relational   51

PART TWO   Happiness At Work   57

7   Everyday Work Happiness   59

8   Developing A Culture Of Happiness   65

9   The Flexibility Conundrum   75

10 How Happy Are You At Work?   81

11 The Danger Of Getting Stuck In OK   89

PART THREE   The Value Of Happiness   93

12 The Inevitable: Unhappy Employees Leave   95

13 How The British Weather Helped Prove
    The Power Of Happiness   105

14 Difficult Customers And Complex Deals   111

15 How Happiness Lowers The Cost Of Sales   117

16 The Magnetic Attraction Of Happiness   123

17 Everyday Creativity And Happiness   129

18 Fired Up Or Burnt Out?   137

19 Double Or Quits   145

20 The Happiness Dividend   153

PART FOUR   Happiness Is A Team Sport   159

21 Teams Are Where The Magic Happens   161

22 Great Teams Are Happy *And* Successful   165

23 Happiness Starts With The Team   173

24 Size Matters, And Shakespeare Knew It   179

25 What Google Got Wrong About
    Team Leaders   185

26 Leading A Team Isn't Easy   193

27 Time: The Currency Of Relationships   197

28 The Seven Successes Of Happy Teams   205

PART FIVE   The Bad And The Ugly   209

29 Three Personal Factors We Often Overlook   211

30 The Cost Of Ignoring Team Happiness   217

31 The Three Ps: Ping-pong, Pizza And Parties   223

32	Most Wellbeing Programmes Don't Work	229
33	Bad Systems Beat Good People	237
34	A Disregard For Managers	243
35	Meaning Isn't Enough	249
36	Humans, Not Resources	257
37	Why Employee Engagement Doesn't Add Up	263
38	Annual Surveys Aren't The Answer	271
39	What Hunter-Gatherers Teach Us About Questionnaire Design	277

PART SIX Building Happy Teams 283

40	Introducing The Dynamic Model Of Team Happiness	285
41	Simple, Three-Step Process For Building Happy Teams	297
42	Measure-Meet-Repeat In More Detail	303
43	Start: Let's Press The Happiness Button	319
44	Time Restraints: The Biggest Obstacle	327

45	How Leaders Can Have Better Conversations	333
46	When To Flip It Around	337
47	A New Focus On Teams	345
Conclusion: Happiness Is The Way		**351**
Bibliography		**359**
Acknowledgements		**369**
The Author		**373**

Preface: From Numbers To People And Numbers About People

I've always been a numbers person. As a child I loved maths and excelled in it without much effort. However, at university I realised I wasn't interested in abstract mathematics. Instead, I wanted to use numbers to solve real-world problems. After graduating from Cambridge, I went on to do a master's degree in operational research – a field we might today call systems thinking. It was fascinating work in queuing theory, simulation modelling and systems dynamics, among many other things. For the first time, I felt like I was using numbers to make a tangible difference.

Numbers alone weren't enough, though. From an early age I'd attended a traditional British boarding school – an environment that wasn't kind to sensitive souls like me. That experience left me keenly aware of the impact of systems on individuals, and after a few years working in consulting, I found myself drawn to the world of self-discovery and personal growth. I started attending workshops and men's groups, and eventually trained as a therapist. That three-year journey taught me a lot about people – their vulnerabilities, their potential and their need for connection. I also learned about the therapeutic process, including how creating a safe space, where people feel able to share their inner experiences, can be powerfully healing. I found working one on one with people a bit lonely, though; I missed working in a team. I therefore decided to try and find a way to combine my love of numbers with my understanding of people, to create change at a larger, systemic level.

Initially, I wasn't sure how I would combine these two strands of my work, but an opportunity arose in 2001 that would change my career – and my life – completely. In the UK policy arena, the word *wellbeing* was gaining traction, and I was asked to do some work on it with a London-based think tank, the New Economics Foundation (NEF). It was the perfect opportunity to combine data and people, by creating data about people and their experience of life. I started off volunteering at the NEF for one day a week, but one thing led to another, and – somewhat accidentally, thanks to a combination of good timing and our rigorous, measurement-led approach – I set up an award-winning research centre!

PREFACE

Over the next decade we completed several groundbreaking projects and worked with local and national governments as well as with international organisations such as the European Statistics Agency and the Organisation for Economic Co-operation and Development. I worked on the questionnaire design team for the European Social Survey, designing their first wellbeing survey across the continent. Based on the data from that survey, we built prototype 'national accounts of wellbeing', showing how wellbeing differed across countries and generations.

In 2006 I created the Happy Planet Index (HPI) – an indicator designed to challenge the use of GDP as a measure of national success. Instead, the HPI measures progress towards a future with sustainable wellbeing where good lives don't cost the earth. For the UK Government of Science we designed the Five Ways to Wellbeing – a practical toolkit for individuals to improve their own positive mental health. That toolkit has since been adopted, and adapted, by multiple public mental health campaigns worldwide.

These were exciting times, learning so much while working with a great team and doing inspiring, impactful work. To top it all, in 2010 I was approached by TED and asked to give a talk at one of their prestigious global conferences. It was a huge privilege to be given a global stage from which to challenge policymakers, and indeed the environmental movement, to take people's wellbeing seriously. It was also a huge pressure, as I knew that this eighteen-minute video was a one-off opportunity. Even though speaking had always been one of my strengths, I worked intensely over several months crafting the talk.

After my TED talk I started to get invites to give keynotes all around the world, and I had a busy couple of years spreading the word. However, over time I started to feel the need to work on something new. Policymaking is a slow process, especially when it comes to environmental challenges. I wanted to do something that created positive change more immediately in people's lives, not just at some point in the future. That's what led me to focusing on the workplace. Work is where we spend a significant portion of our lives. It's where relationships are built, challenges are faced and successes are shared. Unlike national progress, workplace happiness is something we can measure and improve in real time. Happy teams also don't just feel good – they perform better, collaborate more effectively and stay resilient in the face of challenges.

This book is my contribution to bringing the science of happiness to life in the workplace. It's informed by my experience over the last twenty-five years as a statistician, a therapist and a systems thinker. It's shaped by the lessons I've learned from working with thousands of teams across the globe. It's driven by a simple yet powerful belief that happiness is a serious business. That happiness doesn't only feel good but also helps us do good, not just at work but in life as well.

Let me be clear, though: this isn't just another book about happiness. It's not about quick fixes or one-size-fits-all solutions. It's about understanding the dynamics of happiness, personally as well as in teams and organisations, then using that understanding to create lasting positive change. It's about measuring what matters, having meaningful conversations, and building systems that support both well-being and performance.

Introduction: Happiness Is A Serious Business

Happiness at work. To many it might sound like a nice-to-have – a luxury reserved for thriving companies in good times. However, a range of factors – including the pandemic, shifting employee expectations and the rise of hybrid and remote work – mean we are on the threshold of a new era in how we work. It's time to recognise that happiness at work is not just desirable; it's essential. Misunderstood by some as a superficial or even frivolous pursuit, happiness is in fact the foundation of sustainable success. The numbers speak for themselves: happy teams are successful teams, and if you invest in happiness, you invest in success.

The evidence base: Numbers about people

Numbers are important to me, and it's very important to me that numbers are used in the right way.

Happiness at work is a new, evolving field, with exciting research being published all the time. For example, in 2023 the first peer-reviewed article was published that categorically proves that positive moods lead to improved performance in a real business setting (Bellet, de Neve and Ward, 2023). I will guide you through similar fascinating findings throughout the book. I will also draw on my own data, which I have gathered over the last fifteen years. These datasets broadly take two forms:

1. **Representative samples of national working populations.** I have designed and analysed many of these types of surveys from multiple countries, including the USA, the UK, Australia and Canada as well as several other European and Latin American nations.

2. **Longitudinal data tracking the dynamics of weekly team happiness, across thousands of teams.** This data is collected from the clients of my business, Friday Pulse. In this book my analyses are based on trends from 2023 and 2024.

Both types of datasets have pros and cons. The national surveys have the advantage that they are unbiased, but they are snapshots that don't capture the dynamics of happiness. In contrast, the client-based longitudinal data enables the ups and downs of work to be tracked, but they don't cover every sector or geography, so they can't be considered representative. Together, these two different types of datasets provide literally millions of datapoints, and just like numbers and people, they make a powerful combination.

In this book I will use this evidence base to show definitively that happier teams are more successful teams. They're more creative, more productive and more fun to be part of. Building happy teams isn't always easy, though. It requires commitment, curiosity and a willingness to experiment. That's why this isn't just a guide; it's also an invitation. It's an invitation to rethink how we approach work, to challenge old assumptions and to embrace a new way of thinking about success.

The ideas explored here are built on a simple yet transformative premise: happiness is a win-win proposition. Happier employees deliver superior outcomes, from increases in productivity and creativity to reductions in staff turnover and burnout. At the same time, happier workplaces create better experiences for individuals, enriching their lives far beyond the office walls. This dual benefit – superior business results and better lives – makes happiness at work one of the most powerful levers of organisational change.

Some scepticism remains. I've encountered seasoned business leaders who dismiss happiness as irrelevant to performance or, worse, a distraction from 'real work'. Others worry that focusing on happiness might lead to complacency, fearing that happy teams won't be as productive. These concerns highlight how easily happiness is misunderstood in the workplace, but it is not about relentless cheerfulness or constant positivity. It's about fostering environments where people can thrive, where challenges are met with energy and resilience, and where work is a source of pride and purpose.

The data makes the case

Scepticism about happiness at work often stems from outdated assumptions about what drives performance. Some leaders still operate under the belief that stress and pressure are the primary work motivators, pushing employees to perform at their peak.

While it's true that urgency can drive short-term results, the long-term costs – burnout, disengagement and staff turnover – are staggering. A relentless focus on squeezing performance out of teams is not only unsustainable but also counterproductive. Research consistently shows that when people are pushed too hard for too long, their performance suffers.

Research also consistently shows that happier employees are more engaged, more productive and more innovative. Happy employees are 20–30% more productive, with even greater gains in roles that require collaboration, creativity or problem-solving (Whitman et al, 2010).[1] These are not marginal improvements; they are game-changing advantages in a competitive business landscape.

The link between happiness and performance is not anecdotal; it is scientifically robust. Positive emotions – the foundation of happiness – broaden our thinking, making us more creative and adaptable. They build our resilience and our capacity for collaboration, enabling us to rise to challenges with confidence. In contrast, negative emotions narrow our focus, making us less effective and more prone to errors.

The evidence is clear: happiness and performance are not just compatible; they are deeply intertwined.

One of the challenges in promoting happiness at work is its perceived intangibility. What is happiness? How do you act on it? These are questions I've grappled with over my career. The answer lies in measurement – not for the sake of numbers alone but to provide clarity, focus and direction.

In this book I'll introduce you to a systematic, measurement-led approach to building happy teams.

---

1   I will explain how I estimate this figure further in Chapter 13, but it draws on data from a large meta-analysis (Whitman et al, 2010) and applies it to my client data.

This methodology combines regular measurement with team conversations and iterative actions. It's a process that empowers teams to work better together, leading to both happiness and success.

Far from being an abstract ideal, happiness is a practical tool for creating better workplaces. By measuring what matters and taking consistent action, leaders can transform happiness from a soft concept into a strategic advantage. This approach doesn't just make work better; it makes work better in measurable, impactful ways.

I've structured the book as a guide to understanding and applying the science of happiness at work. It's designed to provide both insights and practical tools for anyone passionate about creating a better world of work. Here's what you can expect from the six parts of the book:

1. **Understanding happiness:** We'll explore what happiness is (and isn't), busting myths and uncovering its role as a functional signal that helps us navigate what is and isn't working.

2. **Happiness at work:** We'll look at how happiness manifests in the workplace, not as a vague possibility but in tangible ways, from day-to-day moods to the systemic factors that shape it.

3. **The value of happiness:** You'll discover why happiness isn't a distraction from success

but a driver of it, boosting performance and strengthening relationships.

4. **Happiness is a team sport:** I'll delve into why teams matter more than we realise and how to lead them in ways that support wellbeing and success.

5. **The bad and the ugly:** We'll examine the mistakes organisations sometimes make when addressing happiness and wellbeing, and how to avoid them.

6. **Building happy teams:** I'll outline practical ways to foster team happiness, drawing on the Five Ways to Happiness at Work and my measure-meet-repeat methodology.

If you're reading this, it's because you care about making work better. Whether you're a senior manager or a team leader, an HR professional or a consultant, or if you're simply interested in creating a better world of work, this book is for you. It's a roadmap for applying the science of happiness to the workplace – not as an abstract ideal but as a practical tool for building better teams, organisations and outcomes.

I'm not here to offer you all the answers. All teams and organisations are different, and the right approach will depend on your unique context. What I do offer is a framework, grounded in evidence and experience, that you can adapt to suit your needs. I'll share the tools, stories and insights that have helped thousands of teams improve their happiness and performance. I'll also show you how to measure what matters, so you can track your progress and make informed decisions.

This is my invitation to you: to take what you learn in this book and make it your own. Happiness is serious business, and it's also deeply rewarding. It's about creating workplaces where people can thrive, where challenges are met with energy and creativity, and where success is shared.

By the end of this book, you'll not only understand why happiness matters; you'll also have the tools to make it a reality in your teams and organisations.

PART ONE
UNDERSTANDING HAPPINESS

1
The Inevitable (And Measurable) Ups And Downs Of Happiness

There are many misunderstandings about what happiness is and, in my opinion, at least part of the blame lies with the American Declaration of Independence. It is a hugely inspiring and revolutionary document, but when it declares that we have the 'unalienable right' to 'life, liberty and the pursuit of happiness', it frames happiness as a goal to be pursued and a stable state to be achieved. That sounds great, almost like looking for a beach where you can go and relax, leaving all your unhappiness behind you.

It is true that pursuing a better life, for yourself and your family, is a noble pursuit and even that there is happiness in the pursuit. This doesn't mean you'll be happy all the time, though. It's inevitable that life will have ups and downs; and when things aren't going well, it is appropriate to feel unhappy.

This is an important insight into the biological function of happiness. Feeling happy is a sign that we are a good fit for the environment we find ourselves in – that our inner and outer worlds are aligned. In contrast, unhappiness is a signal that we need to change something. The dynamic between the two acts as a guide, helping us navigate away from environments that aren't good for us. Obviously, we prefer the ups, but this shouldn't come at the cost of ignoring the signals that things aren't going well. Our downs are often where our learnings are.

Happiness during Covid: The rollercoaster first year

Think back to a challenge we all faced not long ago: the pandemic. That whole first year felt a bit of a rollercoaster, didn't it? In the UK we even have a graph that captures this.

The data in that graph, from the British polling agency YouGov, immediately picked up on the impact of the pandemic on how people were feeling. It shows there was a huge drop in happiness in March 2020, as the virus started to spread and its deadly seriousness became apparent. It was a scary time.

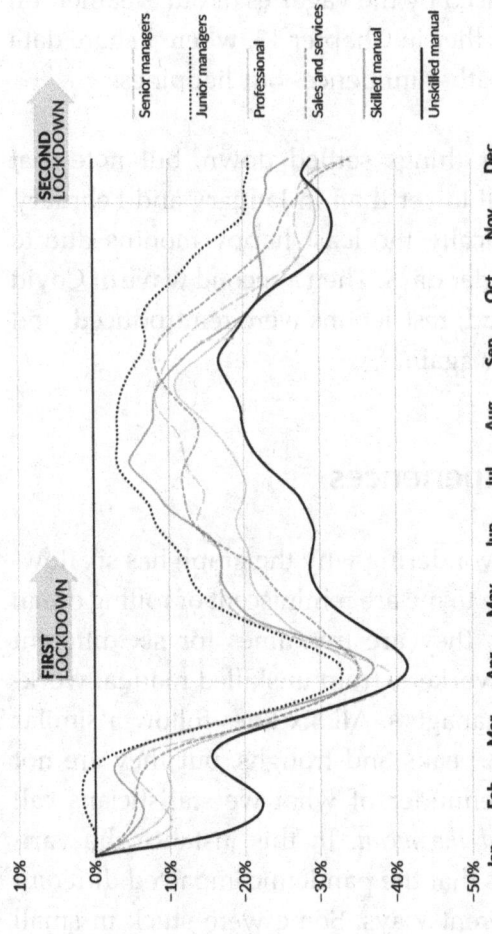

Changes in weekly happiness levels during 2020: UK workers (Source: World Happiness Report 2021, Chapter 7; Data source: YouGov Weekly Mood of the Nation UK)[2]

---

2   The original version of this graph was from Helliwell et al (2021). Professor Jan-Emmanuel de Neve, one of three authors of the *World Happiness Report*, shared this more detailed version with me.

In April and May the graph started to climb back up – a display of resilience as people adjusted to the new restrictions. It most certainly helped that the UK was enjoying a glorious spring, as the mood of us Brits is heavily influenced by the vagaries of our weather! I'll explain this further in Chapter 13, where I share data on how the weather influences our happiness.

In the summer things settled down, but note that levels were still lower than in January and February, which are typically the least happy months due to shorter and colder days. Then a second wave of Covid started to spread, restrictions were reintroduced, and the curve drops again.

Different experiences

You might be wondering why the graph has six flowing lines, which to me are reminiscent of rolling ocean waves. In fact, they are trendlines for six different groups of UK workers, from unskilled manual workers to senior managers. All six lines follow a similar trajectory, with peaks and troughs, but they are not identical – a reminder of what we statisticians call *variation around the mean*. In this instance the variance recognises that the pandemic impacted different people in different ways. Some were stuck in small apartments; others had to try to work from home while homeschooling young children; some people lost loved ones to the virus.

Whenever I share this graph with other people, they respond, *That's how it felt for me.* Strictly, though, it is mapping the weekly average of everyone's experiences throughout the year rather than that of any individual. It is unusual to see such clear patterns like this at a national level, as people's natural ups and downs normally cancel each other out – some will be having a bad week while others are having a good one. During Covid, more people experienced unhappiness at the same time.

The reason we can see the shape of the curve so clearly is because of the frequency of the measurement. If YouGov had decided to measure the mood of the nation only once a year, they would have almost completely missed the impact of Covid. This is one of the major reasons why annual staff surveys aren't the best option. The world of work is fast moving, and annual surveys don't capture the changes.

When you have dynamic data, you can act on it. This became very apparent during the pandemic, with a CEO I work with writing at the time:

> 'Other CEOs can only guess at how lockdown has impacted their employees. I know because we track employee experience every week. At ProSearch we have been able to act on this weekly data, and it has helped us navigate our way through this Covid-19 crisis.'
> – Julia Hasenzahl, CEO ProSearch

Measuring regularly helped Hasenzahl understand what was happening in her teams. She and her senior team were better able to respond to the rapid changes that were needed.

For the UK graph to make sense, it was also critical that YouGov started measuring weekly happiness nearly a year before the pandemic struck, as it was the changes in happiness levels that told the story. This is why I always recommend that teams and organisations measure team happiness regularly on a monthly or weekly basis. Changes in the data can then act as an early warning system, highlighting that something is amiss and needs attention.

The ups and downs of daily life

The data behind the graph above uses perhaps the simplest happiness measure possible: the percentage of people who reported feeling happy in the previous week. When asked *How did you feel this week?*, people could tick several boxes, including one labelled *happy*. Other options included *scared, sad, energetic, frustrated, stressed* and *bored*.

In ongoing surveys, *happy* is ticked most often and is the category that best captures the ups and downs.[3] Interestingly, when I looked more closely at the

---

3   YouGov publishes weekly updates to the data at https://yougov.co.uk/topics/science/trackers/britains-mood-measured-weekly.

YouGov data, it was possible to see that the first dip in the graph above was driven by fear, the second more by boredom. The weekly framing of the question neatly captured the ups and downs of people's lives, but of course these dynamics don't only happen on a weekly basis. It's quite possible to have many different moods in one day.

One recent study set out to explore people's everyday lives by tracking more than 30,000 people's daily experience for over a month (Quoidbach et al, 2019). This wasn't during a global event like the pandemic; instead, the researchers zoomed in to how people's moods and behaviours fluctuated during their everyday lives. One of their general findings was, perhaps unsurprisingly, that people tended to be least happy on the way to work in the morning and most happy when home in the evening.

Much more interesting stories emerged from tracking how individuals' experience changed throughout the day. For example, here are three particularly relevant findings:

1. **Being with other people boosts our happiness.**
   The data shows happy people typically spent twice as much time in the company of others.

2. **Feeling unhappy motivates us to make changes.**
   When people were feeling low, they were twice as likely to call a friend within the next couple of hours.

3. **Feeling happy enables us to rise to challenges.** When people felt good, they were more likely to engage in a challenging task.

The first point above confirms what lots of other studies show, which I will return to repeatedly throughout this book: that relationships are critical to our happiness. This is as true at work as it is in our lives in general.

The second reminds us that we are not passive in our moods – they don't just happen to us. When we feel unhappy, we can take action and improve our mood. In this study it was found that calling a friend was a happiness booster. At work a booster might be taking a break, perhaps having a water-cooler chat with a colleague. Psychologists call this process *self-regulation*, where we are active agents in controlling our moods.

The third is a critical insight, especially for a work context: that when we feel good, we are better able to rise to challenges. Effectively, it is evidence that happiness is more than a good/bad signal. Happiness is also highly functional and gives us energy to work towards achieving challenging goals. I'll return to this topic in the next chapter.

As the pandemic showed, life has its inevitable ups and downs. The graph above shows that these effects are not only inevitable but also measurable. The shape of the curve also captures our natural resilience, that after setbacks we can bounce back. No doubt many of us were employing strategies, such as contacting friends, that helped us cope with the challenges posed by the pandemic.

In our working lives we all have bad weeks. If we quickly bounce back, that is a sign of resilience. If we stay feeling down for long periods, it's a signal that we need to make some changes.

Summary

- **Happiness is a signal, not a goal.** It reflects how well our inner and outer worlds align – when we are a good-fit with our environment, we feel good; when we aren't, unhappiness signals the need for change.

- **Tracking happiness reveals patterns.** Weekly data – like the happiness graph from the first year of Covid – shows how moods shift in response to events. Frequent measurement helps identify misalignments early.

- **Ups and downs can both be functional.** Positive moods energise us to take on challenges; negative moods prompt us to adapt. Recognising this dynamic helps teams navigate uncertainty with greater clarity and resilience.

2
Happiness: More Than A Yellow Emoji

The American Declaration of Independence, issued in 1776, is one source of confusion about happiness. Let's fast-forward a few centuries, and I think we're falling into a different trap of thinking that it's somehow stupid to be happy. That annoying, slightly inane, yellow smiley emoji doesn't help.

I once heard a story about Picasso. He was travelling in a train compartment with another man. The man recognised the artist, and they struck up a conversation. Perplexed by Picasso's paintings, the man asked why he didn't paint people 'as they were'. Picasso, confused, asked the man what he meant. The man took a photograph of his wife out of his wallet and said, 'More like this.' After taking his time to look closely at the photograph, Picasso eventually turned to the man and said, 'Isn't she rather flat and very small?' I feel the same way about the yellow emoji. While it does capture something of feeling positive, it's rather flat and very yellow.

Note: The provenance of this story is at best murky. Perhaps it wasn't Picasso. Perhaps it never took place. No matter – I still like it.

There is a simplicity to happiness, in that it is a sign things are going well. It is also dynamic, highly functional and multifaceted, though, so it's not at all flat. Despite Coldplay's best efforts to elevate the colour, their song 'Yellow' associating it with the highest form of love, happiness is also definitely not always yellow.

What Pixar and Darwin can teach us about emotions

A more nuanced functional popular take on happiness can be found in the first Pixar movie, *Inside Out* (Pixar, 2015). The premise is that an eleven-year-old girl, Riley, has to navigate the emotional challenges of moving to a new city and adjusting to a new life. The way Pixar brings this to life is for her to have characters inside her head: Anger, Fear, Sadness, Disgust and Joy. The film rather delightfully highlights the complexity of emotions and that we need to embrace all feelings, not just the positive ones.

The idea that our emotions are functional has long been recognised by psychologists, with even the great Charles Darwin writing a book on the subject, titled *The Expression of the Emotions in Man and Animals* (Darwin, 1872). He identified a core set of emotions, noting that some were 'low spirit' and others 'high spirit' – a categorisation that remains to this day, though those emotions are now referred to as *negative* and *positive*. This idea was popularised by Paul Ekman, an adviser to Pixar, who in the 1960s and 1970s completed a series of groundbreaking studies. Recent advances in neuroscience suggest that, while emotions may not be as discrete or universal as once thought, the positive/negative distinction remains a powerful and practical one, helping people navigate their emotional lives and make sense of their experiences. For further insight, I recommend Lisa Feldman Barrett's book *How Emotions Are Made* (Feldman Barrett, 2017).

Even *negative* and *positive* labels can lead to confusion, as many people assume that negative emotions are bad for us and must be avoided. While those emotions are more uncomfortable to experience, though, they are highly functional. For example, emotions such as anger and fear form part of our fight-or-flight mechanism, readying us to act in the face of threats. Sadness – another 'negative' emotion – helps us deal with loss and disappointment. It slows us down and helps us reflect on our experience. In *Inside Out* Sadness is really the hero as she teaches Joy, and by extension Riley, that it's OK to feel genuine emotions, even if they are not always positive.

However, just because Riley needed to recognise the value of other emotions doesn't mean that Joy's positivity isn't also highly functional. Her optimism and resilience generate an infectious energy that motivates Riley to engage with the world around her, creatively solving problems and rising to the challenges she faces.

The broaden-and-build theory of positive emotions

The understanding that positive emotions are highly functional had been overlooked by psychologists for a long time, but in the 1990s a young psychologist called Barbara Fredrickson started challenging this omission. She ran a series of innovative, lab-based experiments where she would stimulate the experiencing of positive emotions in a group of people and compare their reactions with those in another group who were in a neutral mood (Fredrickson, 1998). She would set tasks like word association, where participants needed to find one word that linked three other words (for example, the word *power* linking the words *tool*, *atomic* and *foreign*). Other experiments involved scary challenges such as giving an impromptu speech, or more playful ones like building a bridge out of drinking straws and marshmallows.

She concluded that positive emotions were highly functional – that when people felt good, they were more creative and better able to link things together. In another experiment she showed that happier people were also more collaborative, open and flexible. In addition, exposure to positive experiences over time helped build people's confidence, self-esteem and resilience.

Fredrickson proposed that positive emotions had two main functions:

1. They broaden our repertoire of responses to situations.
2. They build our personal resources.

Her findings became known as the *broaden-and-build theory*, which highlighted how – just like their negative counterparts, the fight-or-flight responses – positive emotions have evolved to help us survive and thrive through the millennia (Fredrickson, 2001).

While most of Fredrickson's research was lab-based, her insights are highly relevant to the real world of work. The research highlights that when we feel good, we do good work. This is because we are:

- **More creative** – we are better at generating fresh ideas and solving problems

- **Better decision makers** – we are more open-minded and take a broader perspective

- **More flexible** – we are better able to adapt to changes and recover from setbacks

- **Better colleagues** – we collaborate and support others more

- **More motivated** – we want to reach for more ambitious goals

These are all important reasons for why happiness leads to success, a theme I will keep returning to.

The myth of toxic positivity

Happiness is highly functional, but it is worth remembering that unhappiness is as well. If someone is always too positive, they run the risk of overriding important signals that something is amiss and needs addressing. To others over-positive people can feel inauthentic, ungrounded and not in tune with what is really going on. However, to me this doesn't warrant the use of the term *toxic positivity*. Toxic behaviour is harmful, often involving blame, control and blatant disrespect. Someone being a bit too positive might be annoying, but, unless that is accompanied by other toxic behaviour, it doesn't make others feel unsafe.

In the next chapter I'll outline why it is useful to think of there being two types of happiness: one that helps us maintain stability and one that helps us to embrace change. There is an inherent tension between these two types; however, understanding them can help us create a dynamic balance in our work and lives.

Summary

- **Happiness isn't one-dimensional.** The flat yellow emoji doesn't do justice to the richness and functionality of happiness, which is complex, dynamic and grounded in emotional depth – more Picasso than clipart.

- **Emotions are signals, not noise.** Both positive and negative emotions play vital roles: alerting us to what matters, helping us face challenges and deepening our relationships. They're not distractions; they're data for wiser decisions.

- **Positive emotions broaden and build.** Barbara Fredrickson's research shows that happiness expands our thinking and strengthens our personal resources, boosting creativity, collaboration, flexibility and long-term motivation at work.

3
The Dynamics Of Happiness

Stability and change. We need both in our lives, but too much of either can be a problem. If everything is always change, change, change, we become unsettled and exhausted. If nothing ever changes, things stagnate and we get bored. There is a tension between the two states.

This tension has deep evolutionary roots. All living beings must maintain internal stability to stay alive. They also must interact with an ever-changing external environment. Our feelings and emotions have, at least partially, evolved to help us navigate this tension, with that self-regulation often referred to by biologists as *homeostasis*. Keeping our body temperature, blood pressure and heart rates within certain ranges are all examples of this process. For a wonderful exploration of the evolution of emotions, see Antonio Damasio's book *The Strange Order of Things* (Damasio, 2018).

In the previous chapters I explained that happiness is a sign that we are a good fit with our environment and that happiness and other associated positive emotions are highly functional. In this chapter I will explore the fact that it is helpful to think about there being two different kinds of happiness, and that together they help us create a dynamic balance between our competing needs for stability and change.

Two types of positive emotions

Over the years, more and more research attention has been focused on the power of positive emotions. Perhaps unsurprisingly, given the complexity of emotions, some caveats started to emerge especially to the broaden element of the theory. For example, a positive emotion such as interest explicitly narrows our attention so that we can focus on details. Enthusiasm drives us towards pursuing a goal, but in this mood we are less likely to be open to new ideas. Courage demands that we close ourselves off to hazards and ignore risks.

The idea that some positive emotions broaden our attention and others narrow it might at first appear to be a trivial spat over words. However, the Norwegian psychologist Professor Joar Vittersø, who I have collaborated with on several projects over the decades, proposes that this difference is due to positive emotions activating two different motivation systems: one that maintains stability and one that drives change (Vittersø, 2025). This makes it clear why we have an array of positive emotions and it is useful to differentiate between these two underlying types, which I call *sustaining* and *striving*.

Sustaining

Sustaining emotions such as contentment, tranquillity, safety, caring, lovingness and pleasure help us relax and connect with other people. They are restorative when we are depleted, raising our spirits when we feel low. When we are feeling good in this way, we are more open, which helps us see the bigger picture, enhancing our creativity and making us more flexible. These emotions help us maintain the stability we need, both internally and relationally.

Sustaining emotions are related to what some people call our *rest-and-digest system* (Gilbert, 2009). They are associated with oxytocin, the so-called love hormone that helps us build relationships; and with endorphins, which can make us feel calm. The opposite of feeling sustained is to feel stressed, depleted or isolated.

Striving

Striving emotions help us accomplish tasks and achieve goals. They are sometimes called our drive system. Enthusiasm, excitement and interest all help us mobilise our own energy and that of others. Striving emotions are, to varying degrees, characterised by a narrowing down of attention, which naturally helps us focus on the tasks at hand and to create change.

The hormone most closely associated with these striving emotions is dopamine – sometimes called the *molecule of more*, as it drives our desires (Lieberman and Long, 2019). The opposite of experiencing striving emotions is to feel directionless, disengaged or bored.

Sustaining and striving at work

Striving emotions have a clear link to productivity – they help us focus and achieve goals. It's not surprising that they are much valued in the business world. The quieter, sustaining emotions are just as important, though, as they are related to creativity, resilience and, ultimately, staff retention. They also critically help teams create the psychological safety needed to work well together.[4]

---

[4] Amy Edmondson is recognised as a pioneer of psychological safety (Edmondson, 2018).

Our need for both stability and change means building happy, successful teams is a very dynamic process. Things are always in flux, which can be fun and exciting as well as sometimes quite challenging.

Summary

- **Happiness balances stability and change.** Our emotional lives navigate a fundamental tension between needing consistency and embracing growth. Happiness plays a key role in managing this dynamic.

- **There are two types of positive emotions.** Sustaining emotions (like calmness and connection) restore us and promote flexibility, while striving emotions (like enthusiasm and drive) focus our attention and push us towards goals.

- **Great teams need both types.** While striving fuels productivity and ambition, sustaining emotions support creativity, resilience and psychological safety. Both are essential for long-term success.

4
Boredom Is A Joy Killer

One thing that annoys me as a statistician is that findings are often overstated or overinterpreted, especially by the media. For example, it has been found that people in middle age are less happy than those younger and older than them (Blanchflower and Oswald, 2019). This is often called the U-shaped curve of happiness and is much loved by journalists, as it seems to provide evidence of people having mid-life crises. The figures for the UK show that about 76% of middle-aged people have reasonably good levels of happiness, compared with 79% of those older or younger than them (Office for National

Statistics, 2024).[5] However, while this impact is statistically significant, it is not a large effect. No need to panic if you're middle-aged – it is not compulsory to have a mid-life crisis.

Several statistical methodologies can be used to estimate effect sizes, and in this chapter I am going to use one of these to justify why boredom is more of a joy killer than stress at work. This isn't to say stress is OK – just that boredom is worse.

A good job is interesting but not too stressful

I noticed this effect in the very first dataset I ever analysed on people's experience at work. It was back in 2005, when my work on wellbeing in public policy was starting to gain traction. I was invited by a well-respected UK management group, the Chartered Institute of Personnel Development (CIPD), to contribute to a report they were writing about wellbeing at work. They had commissioned a survey of more than 1,000 employees and kindly gave me access to the raw data.

---

5   This data comes from the UK Labour Force Survey. It is my own analysis, I used data from 2023 and defined a reasonably good level of happiness as those scoring 7 or above on a 0–10 measure of life satisfaction. The Labour Force Survey is conducted every quarter by the Office for National Statistics (ONS).

Excitingly, the survey designers had not only asked about respondents' job satisfaction; they'd also included a set of questions about the respondents' feelings at work, including how exciting, boring, frustrating and stressful they found their jobs (Guest and Conway, 2004). By looking at how these variables interacted with a whole host of other measures such as job satisfaction, work–life balance, and intention to quit, I concluded: A good job is interesting but not too stressful. Effectively, the data showed that only high levels of stress undermined people's experiences at work; moderate levels didn't.

Boredom is four times worse than stress

Over the intervening years, I've often included measures of stress and boredom (or its polar opposite: interest) in my surveys, the most recent one being the 2023 survey I conducted of the UK's working population. The figure below shows the results of a simple linear regression.

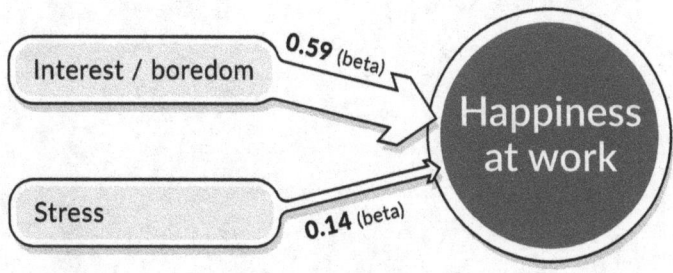

Relative impact of stress and interest on happiness at work

I have shown the beta coefficients from the regression analysis, which indicate the strength of the relationship. The beta coefficient is the value of 'b' in this equation, which you might remember from school: $X = a + bY$

For interest/boredom the beta coefficient is 0.59, which means that for every 1 pt increase in interest, the regression model predicts happiness at work will increase by 0.59 pts (with the opposite effect for any increase in boredom). In contrast, for stress the value is only 0.14. We can conclude that being bored (uninterested) is four times worse for happiness at work than stress.

Of course, this doesn't mean that stress is totally unimportant, and stress at work needs to be actively managed. In the next chapter I will give some tips about dealing with short-term stress, which I learned from an unlikely source: smokers.

Meanwhile, remember that boredom is more of a joy killer than stress.

Summary

- **Boredom is more damaging than stress.** Statistical analysis shows that boredom has a four-times stronger negative impact on workplace happiness than stress, making it a bigger joy killer than many people realise.

- **Moderate stress isn't always harmful.** While high stress needs managing, low to moderate levels don't significantly reduce happiness and may even indicate engagement or challenge.

- **The best jobs are stimulating without being overwhelming.** Data consistently shows that feeling interested and engaged at work is a key driver of happiness – even more so than avoiding stress.

5
A Lesson From Smokers

I want to give you a tip for when you feel stressed, especially when you experience the short-term stress that comes from an everyday frustration or from working too intensely for a few hours.

When you find yourself in this situation, think what a smoker would do! (I am not suggesting that smoking is healthy, but some of the behaviours of smokers are great stress-busting strategies.)

Regular breaks

Smokers are good at taking regular breaks. They get up from their desks, move their bodies and go outside into the daylight, all of which is great for relieving the tension that has been building up. Taking a five-minute break every hour is good for us.

On each break, smokers chat with their fellow smokers, which lifts their mood. As someone who has always been a non-smoker, I used to be jealous of how smokers would go up to a stranger and ask for a light. I'm sure they often had matches in their pocket but had a great excuse to kickstart a conversation.

Mindful breathing

It's always struck me how 'blissed out' smokers look as they intensely inhale and exhale. Basically, they are practising mindful breathing, albeit with lots of carcinogens thrown in.

The trick with mindful breathing is to slow down your breathing and exhale for a little longer than you inhale, for example:

- Inhale for four seconds
- Exhale for six to eight seconds

Some people suggest that the benefit comes less from breathing out for longer and more from pausing between the in and out breaths. Either way, your mind automatically calms, and you relax. You have activated the parasympathetic nervous system, which promotes relaxation. In our evolutionary past, this probably happened after we had escaped danger and were catching our breath. It is a signal that all is safe now.

Putting this advice together into an easy-to-remember mnemonic gives us:

- S – Stop what you're doing
- M – Move your body, and go ...
- O – Outside
- K – Kickstart conversations
- E – Exhale longer than you inhale
- R – Relax

Summary

- **Smokers instinctively manage stress well.** They take regular short breaks, move their bodies, get fresh air and connect with others – healthy habits disguised by an unhealthy one.
- **Mindful breathing really works.** Slowing the breath, especially extending the exhale, activates the body's natural relaxation response and helps regulate stress.
- **The SMOKER mnemonic helps.** Stop, Move, go Outside, Kickstart conversations, Exhale longer, and Relax – a memorable way to de-stress without picking up a cigarette.

6
Happiness Is Deeply Relational

'Happiness is almost a social emotion' is a quote I attribute to the late – and most certainly great – Daniel Kahneman. Best known for winning the Nobel Prize for Economics in 2002, Kahneman was one of the world's most influential thinkers. He had an extraordinary ability to fully commit to ideas, while remaining open to changing his mind when evidence demanded it. That rare combination – of conviction and curiosity – meant he never stopped wrestling with complex questions. His observation about happiness being 'almost a social emotion' captures a subtle but powerful truth: that our happiness is deeply shaped by our relationships with others.

In his best-selling book *Thinking, Fast and Slow* (Kahneman, 2012), he differentiated between two modes of human thinking:

1. **System one** – fast and instinctive, more unconscious, emotionally based
2. **System two** – slower and deliberative, more reflective and cognitive

This powerful insight is genuinely useful when it comes to thinking about the role of happiness in our lives. When we feel happy or unhappy, we are drawing predominantly on our system-one thinking. While system one is prone to some biases, it provides an exceptionally useful first approximation of what is happening. In contrast, system-two thinking is more effortful. It is when we step back and analyse the situation more thoroughly. This reminds us that it is important to not slavishly follow our feelings, but to consider them as useful information to reflect on.

Happiness is social

While happiness is often viewed as a personal or internal experience, it is also profoundly social. It arises in relationships – with others, and with the systems we are embedded in. Our moods ripple outward, shaping those around us, just as their moods shape us in return.

Psychologists typically classify emotions like empathy, jealousy, gratitude, shame and love as 'social emotions' – those that help us build and maintain relationships. Happiness isn't usually included in this list, yet it behaves in a similar way. It thrives on connection, is reinforced by reciprocity, and deepens through shared experience. In this sense, happiness may not be a classic social emotion, but it is certainly a relational one. That makes it central not just to life but to work too.

Friend or foe? A revealing instant judgement

Our ability to quickly judge whether a stranger is friend or foe is a classic example of Kahneman's system-one thinking – fast, intuitive, and automatic. After just a couple of seconds, we have a 'good' or 'bad' feeling about the other person. This assessment is surprisingly accurate, with one study showing that from just three two-second video clips of teachers at work, strangers accurately predicted how they were rated by their supervisors and students (Ambady and Rosenthal, 1993).

These rapid social assessments are based predominantly on two factors: warmth and competence. In other words: does the unknown person intend us good or ill, and then can they act on their intentions? The scariest combination has to be that they intend to harm us and are competent (Fiske, Cuddy and Glick, 2007).[6] We assess people in this order, with the warmth signal picked up first, closely followed by the competence signal. I'll return to this combination when I explore the qualities needed for people to be good leaders; for now it is a reminder that people skills are essential, and they are as important as technical skills when it comes to leading teams.

Our ability to make an instinctive and almost instant friend/foe judgement has deep evolutionary roots. Making friends, collaborating and building allegiances have been a critical element in our evolutionary success as a species. In fact, it wouldn't be too much of a stretch to say that building relationships is our superpower. The British psychologist Robin Dunbar puts this down to what he calls our *social brain* (Dunbar, 1992). He proposes that the reason we developed complex brains, particularly our super-sized neocortices, was due to the demands of living in social groups. We have used our ingenuity and collaborative skills to solve complex problems together and thrive as a species.[7]

This is as true today at work as it has been in our evolutionary past, and collaboration is fundamental to building happy and successful teams.

---

6   For an excellent summary, see page 23 of Joar Vittersø's book *Humanistic Wellbeing* (Vittersø, 2024).
7   See also *The Social Brain* (Camilleri, Rockey and Dunbar, 2024).

Summary

- **Happiness is deeply relational.** While often seen as an individual feeling, happiness is profoundly influenced by our social interactions, both shaping and being shaped by the people around us.

- **Our social instincts run deep.** From split-second friend-or-foe judgements to our desire for warm, competent connections, our brains are wired to assess and prioritise relationships.

- **Collaboration is our superpower.** Evolved for group living, humans thrive – at work and in life – through connection. Investing in relationships is essential for building happy, successful teams.

PART TWO
HAPPINESS AT WORK

7
Everyday Work Happiness

What's a great day at work for you? If you're like most people, a great day is when there are challenges, but you can rise to them. Sometimes we get so absorbed in a task that we almost lose track of time; it's a wonderful feeling. Psychologists call this sensation *flow*. Tennis players get into the zone. Musicians get lost in the music. For statisticians like me, it's Excel spreadsheets that we get immersed in!

The famous Hungarian-American psychologist Mihaly Csikszentmihalyi (pronounced *Chick-sent-me-high-ly*) first coined this idea of flow in the 1970s, which he later wrote about in his seminal book *Flow* (Csikszentmihalyi, 1990). His research has shown that we experience flow when the challenges we face are well matched to our skill levels. This highlights that there is a point when challenges can become overwhelming, resulting in us becoming highly stressed. At the other end of the scale, where things are too easy, we are at risk of getting bored.

Happiness and success go hand in hand when we're in flow, but it is important to seek the sweet spot. Finding flow is about optimisation, not maximisation. When things get too much, both our happiness and performance will drop. In fact, it will be our feelings that first bring our attention to the fact that we are getting out of balance. This is why listening to our feelings can be helpful. They act like an early warning system, providing us with information about whether we are a good fit in the environment we are in, and helping us respond to the ups and downs we face.

Not all downs are inevitable

While it is inevitable that life will have ups and downs, not all downs are inevitable. In our work lives there are often frustrations, many of which are avoidable. One person who has studied their impact is the renowned psychologist Professor Teresa Amabile from Harvard Business School. In a frankly heroic study she, together with colleagues, collected daily diaries from 238 participants from seven different organisations over a six-month period. In their diaries respondents recorded notes at the end of each day about their daily experience of work. They also answered questions about what Amabile called their *inner work life* – effectively, their daily mood at work. Amabile and her colleagues tenaciously managed to achieve a 75% response rate across the whole study, collecting a total of more than 12,000 daily reports for their analysis. It is an impressive and insightful study.

The findings were published in a series of papers as well as a book called *The Progress Principle* (Amabile and Kramer, 2011). The book's title makes the main finding clear: people felt happiest when they were progressing their work, what she called *small wins*, and least happy when they suffered setbacks or frustrations.

To use an analogy from engineering: setbacks are like friction, whereas progress is like flow. Whether at an individual or organisational level, work runs more smoothly and more successfully when friction is reduced and flow increases. My own research, though, shows there is a lot of friction in people's working weeks.

Daily frustrations hold us back

In early 2023 I carried out a representative survey of the UK working population, which included some questions about people's weekly experience. One of those questions was: What was the most frustrating thing about your work this week?

Most people reported experiencing frustrations, with the five most cited ones being:

1. Interpersonal conflicts with manager or colleagues (23%)

2. Poor systems, especially IT and admin systems (23%)

3. Overload – either personal workload or staffing issues (19%)

4. Physical or mental health issues – fatigue, stress, etc (19%)

5. Customer and client interactions (15%)

There are always going to be challenges at work, but there is clearly a lot of room for removing many of these sources of friction. They hold people back from doing their best work and from feeling happier at work.

Professor Amabile's work got into the detail of people's working lives and shows comprehensively that people enjoy progressing their work and hate getting held back. Her in-depth study was of just seven organisations, and my own research, which tracks happiness in thousands of teams across hundreds of organisations, confirms how prevalent frustrations are for people on a weekly basis.

Understanding people's everyday experience of work reveals perhaps one of the most unrecognised ways of becoming happier at work, which is simply by reducing daily frustrations. Less friction, more flow.

Summary

- **Flow fuels happiness and performance.** When challenges match our skill level, we enter a state of flow, where we feel both engaged and successful. Finding this sweet spot is key to everyday satisfaction at work.

- **Not all downs are inevitable.** While life has natural ups and downs, many daily frustrations at work are avoidable. Research shows that setbacks (friction) undermine happiness, while progress (flow) boosts it.

- **Less friction leads to better flow.** From clunky systems to poor communication, everyday frustrations hold people back. Removing these barriers is a practical and often overlooked way to improve happiness at work.

8
Developing A Culture Of Happiness

'Culture eats strategy for breakfast' is a quote widely attributed to Peter Drucker, the renowned management consultant. Whether or not he said it in those precise words, it's a great turn of phrase. It neatly encapsulates the fact that the success or failure of an organisation's strategies are often down to the way people work together. Happiness is more about *we* than *me*.

However, the definition of culture is a bit of a mystery. Some people use other words like *atmosphere*, *climate*, *environment*, *mindset* or *values*. Those terms have slightly different emphases, but all boil down to how people work together. What I like about *culture* is that it is neutral – you can have good and bad cultures, and everything in between. Drucker himself never provided a definition, while the UK's CIPD says:

'Despite its dominance, the language of culture is often unclear and difficult to define, meaning it is also hard to measure. Consequently, real culture change is near-impossible if we can't actually pin down what we're looking to change.' (CIPD, no date)

Typically, most definitions of culture are wordy and emphasise things like shared values, beliefs and norms. I like the simplicity of one popular definition: *The way we do things around here*. It's a reminder that work cultures are revealed in how teams and organisations actually behave.

My simple definition is therefore: A great culture enables people and teams to be happy and successful.

I like this definition as it is tangible and has a clear goal – to be happy and successful. A culture with clear, measurable outcomes also has the advantage that its drivers can be identified statistically, which was key to me creating what I call the Five Ways to Happiness at Work – five positive actions that help people thrive at work.

The Five Ways to Happiness at Work

The Five Ways to Happiness at Work is a model that promotes good work. Over the years, many academics and thinkers have proposed theories, conducted experiments and analysed data about good work. Perhaps most famously, Abraham Maslow proposed his hierarchy of needs, from physical needs at the base of the pyramid to self-actualisation at the top (Maslow, 1943). Other models and theories use different words or place different emphases, but they all cover similar ground.[8]

My Five Ways model clearly overlaps with many of these ideas – inevitably so, since we're all circling the same aim: how to make work truly work for people. In my opinion, you should be suspicious if someone says they have a completely new theory, as we are all addressing the same goal: good work.

The key difference with the Five Ways is how they are framed, with the main aim being to make the model easier to relate to and put into action.[9] Instead of using dry, academic terms like *relatedness, justice, autonomy, development* or *purpose*, I have 'messaged' the Five Ways as positive actions, as illustrated below.

---

[8] The hierarchical nature of Maslow's theory is widely challenged nowadays, but it remains a classic touchstone. Ed Deci and Rich Ryan's self-determination theory proposed three needs: relatedness, autonomy and competence (Deci and Ryan, 1980). Daniel Pink's book *Drive* (Pink, 2011) was probably partially inspired by them – his three factors were autonomy, mastery and purpose. Martin Seligman, the founder of the positive psychology movement, proposed a five factor model called PERMA: Positive emotions, Engagement, Relationships, Meaning, Accomplishment (Seligman, 2011). Less well known is the thorough work of British psychologist Peter Warr (Warr, 2011) and more recently Professor Jan-Emmanuel de Neve of Oxford University (De Neve and Ward, 2025).

[9] My colleagues and I first used these ideas when writing 'The Five Ways to Wellbeing' (Aked et al, 2008).

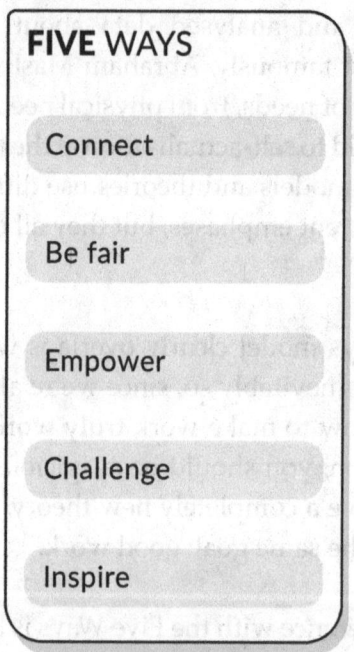

Five Ways to Happiness at Work

These link back to the two types of positive emotions: sustaining and striving. The first two of the Five Ways, *connect* and *be fair*, are more about sustaining; the other three about striving. Underneath these headline words are a whole myriad of possibilities, as there are many ways to fulfil the Five Ways.

The Five Ways are invitations to try out new ways of working rather than as commands to be put into action. In my experience, happiness and wellbeing are best promoted by coaching and facilitation as opposed to a more prescriptive approach.

Let's look in more detail at each of the Five Ways:

1. **Connect – friendships, laughter, a sense of belonging.** It is much easier to do great work when we are happy in the company of others. Teams who encourage, support and appreciate each other make problem-solving, innovation and success possible.

2. **Be fair – flexibility, appreciation, space for people's life outside work.** Being treated with fairness and respect is fundamental to happier work. People flourish when organisations are responsive to their needs and value the energy they put in. Teams flourish when colleagues appreciate one another.

3. **Empower – trust, delegation, the opportunity to self-organise.** Sharing responsibility and playing to people's strengths can unleash amazing potential in the workplace. When people are able to be themselves and use their judgement, they do great work.

4. **Challenge – stretch, learning, realistic expectations.** People are happy in their jobs when they are absorbed and progressing in their work. By making jobs interesting, organisations pull people into a space where they learn and achieve great things.

5. **Inspire – pride, purpose, being part of a bigger picture.** Doing a job that we feel is genuinely worthwhile is a great source of motivation in our lives, and it can sustain us through challenging times. Work becomes more meaningful when we can see beyond narrow business goals to how we help other people.

The Five Ways are all interconnected and often impact each other. If you have good connections with your colleagues, you will find it easier to rise to challenges and learn new things. When we are treated fairly, we feel empowered to do our best work. Clearly the opposites can also be true. When our work is uninspiring, we don't feel like rising to challenges. There can be occasions when a deficit in one area is offset by another; for example, when we feel we are being treated unfairly, we might build stronger relationships at work to cope.

The Five Ways to Happiness at Work model helps us understand the key drivers of happiness at work. The Five Ways demystify what a good workplace culture is – if people have opportunities to experience them, those people will not only feel good, but they will also do good work.

A Five Ways lens on classic business ideas

The Five Ways to Happiness at Work model offers a holistic approach, allowing for the use of many additional approaches. Over the years, many classic business books have been written in this area, and in the list below I have chosen the fifteen I have found most helpful. You'll find three for each of the Five Ways, listed alphabetically rather than in order of preference:

- **Connect:**
  - *Give and Take* (Grant, 2014)
  - *The Social Brain* (Camilleri, Rockey and Dunbar, 2024)
  - *The Song of Significance* (Godin, 2023)

- **Be fair:**
  - *Appreciative Inquiry* (Cooperrider and Whitney, 2005)
  - *The Fearless Organization* (Edmondson, 2018)
  - *It Doesn't Have to Be Crazy at Work* (Fried and Hansson, 2018)

- **Empower:**
  - *Delivering Happiness* (Hsieh, 2010)
  - *Drive* (Pink, 2011)
  - *The 7 Habits of Highly Effective People* (Covey and Covey, 2020)

- **Challenge:**
  - *Radical Candor* (Scott, 2017)
  - *The Fifth Discipline* (Senge, 2006)
  - *The Progress Principle* (Amabile, 2011)

- **Inspire:**
  - *Conscious Capitalism* (Mackey and Sisodia, 2013)
  - *Let My People Go Surfing* (Chouinard, 2006)
  - *Start With Why* (Sinek, 2011)

That was a hard list to choose, and I expect you have some different ones. Regardless, the Five Ways show that there are many potentially good starting points for promoting happiness at work.

The Five Ways framework highlights the approaches that drive both happier and more successful work. In the next chapters I'll illustrate how the Five Ways methodology can be used to address complex challenges. I'll focus first, in Chapter 9, on one of the biggest conundrums in the modern workplace: working from home and the increased demand for flexibility.

Summary

- **Culture is how people work together.** A great culture isn't about slogans or perks; it's about shared behaviours that enable teams to be both happy and successful. It's measurable and manageable, and it shapes outcomes at least as much as strategy.

- **The Five Ways will help you find new ways of working.** Connect, Be fair, Empower, Challenge and Inspire offer a clear, actionable framework for promoting happiness through everyday team practices, grounded in robust psychological and organisational theory.

- **Abstract ideals can be transformed into practical action.** The Five Ways translate broad values into specific behaviours and choices, helping organisations build cultures where people feel good and do great work, not just in theory, but in daily reality.

9
The Flexibility Conundrum

Flexible working is one of the hottest topics in organisations today, sparking heated debates in offices, on Zoom calls and during dinner table conversations. On the surface, the point seems simple: people want autonomy over where and how they work. Who wouldn't? If you look beyond the immediate, though, the issue is far more complex.

The Five Ways can provide a useful framework for thinking through the full implications of complex challenges such as the increasing demand for working from home. Let's look first, though, at some figures on the scale of the changes that have happened since the pandemic. They are quite dramatic.

The graph below shows data from the US that illustrates the working-from-home trend from 1965 to 2025. The vertical axis shows the percentage of all paid workdays that were worked at home.

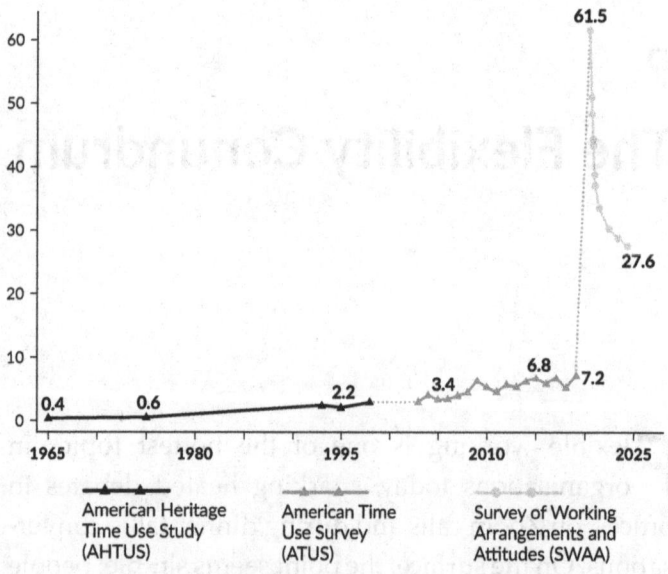

Figures for the number of full days worked at home (USA, 1965–2025) (Source: SWAA March 2025, Updates Barrero et al, 2025)

The UK shows a similar pattern, with 28% of people working in a hybrid way as of October 2024 (Office for National Statistics, 2024). While there's no exact pre-pandemic comparator for hybrid work, the same survey found that an additional 12% of people were working fully from home – more than double the 5% who did so before the pandemic.

What is clear is that the world of work has changed. The pandemic greatly accelerated a rising trend in working from home. However, that doesn't mean there aren't complex trade-offs for individuals, teams and organisations. Here's where a Five Ways perspective can help:

1. **Connect:** We often underestimate the importance of everyday social moments – shared experiences, informal chats and spontaneous laughter – until they vanish. Remote work can lead to disconnection and loneliness. When designing flexible working policies, it's essential to consider how they affect trust, relationships and team cohesion.

2. **Be fair:** Flexibility can help people feel respected and supported, especially when they are balancing complex lives. It's not available to everyone, though – some roles require physical presence. If not handled with care, flexible work can create inequalities and resentment. Even the flexibility itself can backfire if boundaries blur and people feel they're 'always on'.

3. **Empower:** The ability to choose when and where to work can be deeply empowering. It gives people a sense of control over their time and energy, yet autonomy must come with visibility. Remote workers risk being overlooked for opportunities, recognition and development

unless systems are in place to ensure they're not out of mind when out of sight.

4. **Challenge:** Working from home can be great for deep focus, but it also limits access to informal learning – those unplanned conversations that spark insight or help someone grow. Junior staff, in particular, benefit from proximity to mentors and real-time feedback. The challenge is to ensure that flexibility doesn't come at the cost of development.

5. **Inspire:** Fulfilment at work isn't just about what we do – it's about meaning, shared purpose and celebrating success together. Flexible working should support these goals, not undermine them. The best approaches help people stay connected to the bigger picture and to one another, no matter where they're working.

As illustrated here, the Five Ways to Happiness at Work model provides a fresh perspective and encourages us to look beyond the obvious. The rising demand for flexibility is understandable, but the resulting complexities often aren't fully appreciated. Flexible working isn't just about *where* we work; it also impacts *how* we work. By using the Five Ways as a framework, these deeper dynamics can be more fully understood.

There's no one-size-fits-all answer to the flexibility challenge. Every workplace is different – shaped by what kind of work it does, where it's based, and the lives and needs of the people who work there.

In the next chapter I am going to turn the spotlight onto you and your current happiness at work. I will also introduce you to the Five Ways survey, which I use with teams and organisations.

Summary

- **Flexible working has transformed expectations.** The post-pandemic shift towards hybrid and remote work is here to stay, but it introduces complex trade-offs that go far beyond location.

- **The Five Ways reveal hidden tensions.** Flexibility can empower individuals and support wellbeing, but if not designed carefully, it can also erode connection, fairness, visibility and learning.

- **There's no single answer.** Every team must navigate its own balance, one that supports both happiness and performance. The Five Ways provide a framework to achieve it.

10
How Happy Are You At Work?

In this chapter I will give you an experience of reflecting on your own happiness at work, using the Five Ways as a framework, which is useful for two reasons:

1. It will hopefully help you relate better to the Five Ways.

2. As the airlines always say, you should apply your own oxygen mask before helping others. If you aren't happy at work, it will be harder for you to help others.

I could get very technical on how to create measures of the Five Ways, but I'll stick with a brief overview for now. The Five Ways were identified by narrowing the drivers, using a combination of regressions, correlations and factor-structure analysis. Early questionnaires had more than 100 questions, which were slowly narrowed down to the current fifteen. There are five subscales, each with three questions. A three-item scale is considered the shortest possible scale you can achieve and test for internal consistency.

The good news is that there are only fifteen questions to answer – three for each of the Five Ways. I have learned, the hard way, that keeping questionnaires short is the best for collecting robust data, as nobody likes wading through hundreds of questions.[10]

You can either answer the questions below or scan the QR code or visit https://nicmarks.org/whq to complete the online version, which will generate a personalised report for you.

---

10 To my shame, the first wellbeing questionnaire I designed, in 2002, had over 150 questions, and I was asking those of school kids. I can only apologise to them! I simply didn't know what I was doing, but I learned a lot. That questionnaire became the basis of my first wellbeing report (Marks, 2004).

The Five Ways questionnaire

		1	2	3	4	5
Connect	How well do you get along with people in your team?	< Not at all				Very much so >
	Do you feel that teams within your organisation generally work well together?	< Not at all				Very much so >
	Do you feel that you have good friends at work?	< Not at all				Very much so >
Be fair	Do you feel satisfied with the balance between your work and the other aspects of your life?*	< Not at all				Very much so >
	Do you feel that you are treated with fairness and respect at work?	< Not at all				Very much so >
	How appreciated do you feel for your efforts at work?*	< Not at all				Very much so >

The Five Ways questionnaire (continued)

Empower	Do you feel free to be yourself at work?	1 < Not at all	2	3	4	5 Very much so >
	How often do you get to use your strengths in your job?	1 < Not at all	2	3	4	5 Very much so >
	Do you feel you can influence important decisions in your work?	1 < Not at all	2	3	4	5 Very much so >
Challenge	How often do you receive helpful feedback on your performance?	1 < Not at all	2	3	4	5 Very much so >
	How often do you get the chance to be creative in your job?	1 < Not at all	2	3	4	5 Very much so >
	Do you feel that you are learning new things at work?	1 < Not at all	2	3	4	5 Very much so >
Inspire	Do you feel a sense of accomplishment from your work?	1 < Not at all	2	3	4	5 Very much so >
	Do you feel the work you do is worthwhile?	1 < Not at all	2	3	4	5 Very much so >
	Do you feel proud to work for your organisation?	1 < Not at all	2	3	4	5 Very much so >

Your score

If you use the online version, you'll receive more detailed analysis, but I'll keep things simple here:

Simply add up how many of the fifteen questions you answered positively, ie with a score of 4 or 5. This will give you a score of between 0 and 15.

- If you answered positively to thirteen or more questions, you are among the happiest 20% of the working population.
- If you answered 9–12 questions positively, you are reasonably happy at work, though there is room for improvement in some specific areas.
- If you answered 4–8 questions positively, you are probably just OK at work. It would be good to look at your lower scores and seek to address them.
- If you answered 3 or fewer positively, you are probably struggling with your current role. You are in the lowest 20%, and there is a lot to address.

Whatever your scores, it is good to take some time to reflect on your results. Here are some questions you can ask yourself:

- What pleases me most about my highest scores?

- How might I positively influence my lower scores?
- Who can support me in improving my experience of work?

You might also have wondered what the asterisks next to work–life balance and appreciation mean. If you have scored a 1 or 2 on either of these, or a 3 on both, take care – these are the two biggest predictors of burnout. If you are working long hours and don't feel appreciated for your efforts, over time your work is likely to grind you down. My recommendation would be to actively seek to get back into a healthier balance as soon as possible.

The Five Ways as a measure of team culture

When I work with teams and organisations, I get everyone to complete the Five Ways questionnaire at the same time. The collated results help them identify areas of strengths and opportunities for improvement in their workplace.

The Five Ways provide an easy-to-understand framework and a shared language for teams to reflect on how they work together. Crucially, they point towards a goal that everyone can embrace: to be both happier and more successful at work. This is the power of a happiness-led approach – it aligns what individuals genuinely value with what organisations need. Rather than treating happiness as a side issue or a nice-to-have, the Five Ways show that when people thrive, performance improves too. It's a win-win, and a compelling reason to take happiness at work seriously.

Summary

- **The Five Ways questionnaire helps improve happiness at work.** This is a quick, fifteen-question tool to reflect on your own experience of work, using the Five Ways framework.

- **The questionnaire highlights strengths and opportunities.** Your score highlights where you're thriving and where you might need support, especially in areas linked to burnout.

- **The questionnaire measures team culture.** When used across a team, the Five Ways provide shared language and data to understand and improve how people work together.

11
The Danger Of Getting Stuck In OK

When we are happy, we feel positively energised and ready to create and seize opportunities – to broaden and build, as Barbara Fredrickson called it.

When we are unhappy, we can also feel energised, but our energy is then demanding that we take action to avoid threats. This is our fight-or-flight response mechanism, which can be destructive at work.

What about the times when we are neither happy nor unhappy, when we just feel OK? These can be the times we feel the lowest amount of energy. Things are passable, but we lack vibrancy and motivation. This middle ground can be deceptive: nothing feels wrong enough to require immediate action, but nothing feels truly right either.

Stuck in OK

It is all too easy to get stuck in OK, which can be dangerous. We can get stuck in OK relationships in life, which aren't fulfilling but also aren't terrible. When it comes to our physical health, we can get stuck in OK too – perhaps our lifestyles aren't healthy, but things aren't bad enough to force us into making changes.

It's the same at work, where we can easily get stuck in OK jobs. They aren't bad enough that we have to change, yet they aren't great either, which can gradually wear us down. This isn't only a personal issue; it's an organisational risk. Teams that are mostly OK report lower collaboration, creativity and productivity.

In my data I can see evidence of individuals and teams getting stuck in OK. For example, only 20% of teams that are OK in one quarter rate themselves as happy in the next. This matters, as OK teams are more likely to miss their targets and also have significantly higher staff turnover rates. I'll delve deeper into these figures later, but in short: teams that are OK are at about twice as much risk of underperformance as happy teams and have about a 50% higher staff turnover rate.

What causes people and teams to get stuck in OK? Typically, the answer isn't a single issue but a lack of positives. When people feel OK, they often report neutral responses across several areas rather than having specific negatives. They're not actively unhappy but feel that few things are working well. This 'neutral zone' can be flat but persistent, with people surviving but not thriving.

How to get unstuck

If you or your team feels stuck in OK, the best way to escape is by understanding the drivers of happiness at work. The Five Ways questionnaire can help by identifying specific areas for improvement. Any poor scores clearly need to be addressed. However, being stuck in OK is often characterised by lots of neutral scores, so my advice to you and your team is to:

- **Consider neutral zones.** Identify the neutral aspects of work. Perhaps collaboration is fine but not energising, or feedback is helpful but not inspiring. These areas are often ripe for improvement, and enhancing them can have an outsized impact on overall happiness.

- **Identify potential small wins.** In the transition from OK to happy, small positive shifts often make a big difference. Focusing on improving a few key areas will allow you to move out of OK more reliably. Simple practices like setting small, achievable goals can create momentum for change.

- **Appreciate progress.** Recognising accomplishments, even small ones, helps us see that we are moving forward. Acknowledging progress not only boosts happiness but also motivates further improvement, creating a positive feedback loop.

We need to be aware that OK isn't really OK. If we ignore the risks of OK, then mediocrity becomes the norm, which at work risks considerable underperformance.

While it requires effort to shift from only being OK, the benefits are clear: we are not only happier; we are also more likely to be successful too.

Summary

- **OK is a risky middle ground.** When we're not happy or unhappy but just fine, we often lack the energy or urgency to make changes, yet this state can quietly erode motivation and performance.

- **OK teams underperform.** Data shows that OK teams are significantly more likely to miss targets and face higher staff turnover. Stuckness isn't always caused by problems; it's often due to a lack of positives.

- **Getting unstuck means taking action.** Use the Five Ways to identify areas of neutral experience, focus on small wins, and celebrate progress to shift from surviving to thriving.

PART THREE
THE VALUE OF HAPPINESS

12
The Inevitable: Unhappy Employees Leave

It is obvious that staff retention is linked to happiness at work. Being unhappy is a signal to change, and in the workplace that often means changing jobs. I am certain that most organisations underestimate the costs of staff turnover, so in this chapter I will explore these costs in more detail.

Happiness boosts staff retention

There is overwhelming evidence that happiness boosts staff retention. In a report for the wonderfully named Global Happiness Council, researchers carried out a meta-analysis that drew on 339 different research studies with more than 1.8 million employees (Helliwell et al, 2019). Big data! It showed that staff turnover was just as strongly negatively correlated to employee wellbeing as productivity was positively correlated. The careful analysis looked at the impact within sectors, which is important as there are large differences in staff turnover between them. For example, hospitality has a turnover rate of about 50%, whereas the public sector's turnover rate is much lower at about 15% (Bureau of Labor Statistics, 2024).[11]

In my data I see the same impact, and I find the clearest way of showing it is to compare the turnover rates for the unhappy, OK and happy employees. Below are two charts showing the relationship. At the top, data from one large global business with 9,000 employees shows how happiness in one quarter predicts staff turnover in the next quarter.[12] The lower graph is from a series of representative samples of eight nations from a survey I conducted with the global recruitment agency Robert Half. It involved more than 22,000 workers, and included in the survey was a question asking about their intention to quit within the next six months.

---

11 These are median US figures from the US Bureau of Labor. In the UK there aren't official statistics on tenure by sector, but the British Labour Force Survey has tenure bands, which roughly align with the US figures. Note: annual turnover rate = 1/{length of tenure}.

12 Happiness was measured in quarter one, then the actual staff turnover rate was observed in the next quarter. The client was a global currency exchange business and the analysis was carried out by my long-term colleague Dr Saamah Abdallah.

THE INEVITABLE: UNHAPPY EMPLOYEES LEAVE

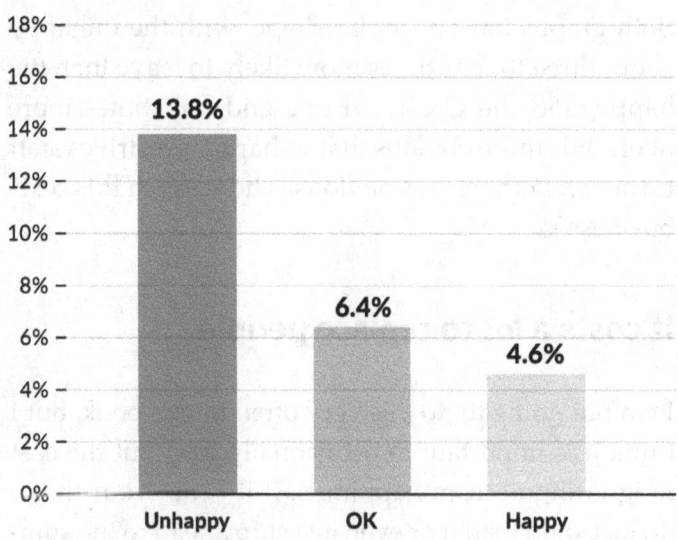

*Happiness and staff turnover
(9,000 employees at one company)*

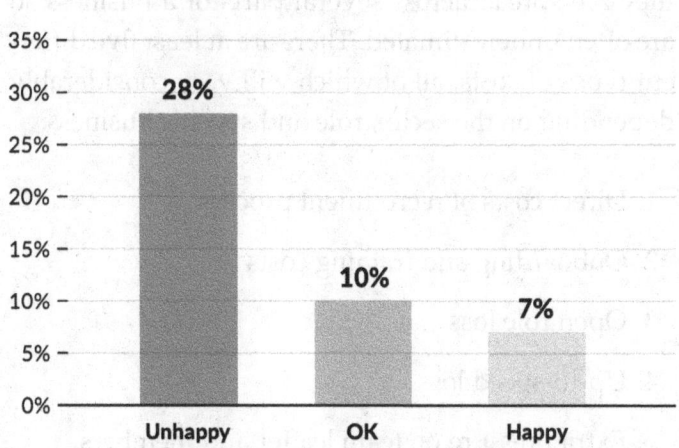

*Happiness and intention to quit
(22,000 employees across 8 nations)*

Both graphs have a similar shape, with the unhappy about three to four times more likely to leave than the happy, and the OK about one and half times more likely. It is quite obvious that unhappiness drives staff turnover. Perhaps less obvious is how much this costs businesses.

It costs a *lot* to replace people

I am not going to do this very often in this book, but I think it is important to occasionally cash out the cost of ignoring of team happiness. If it is not your thing, do just skim read it or even just skip ahead to the summary points at the end of the chapter.

One of the issues with the costs of recruitment is that they are spread across several parts of a business so are often underestimated. There are at least five different types of costs, all of which will vary considerably depending on the sector, role and specific business:

1. Direct costs of recruitment process
2. Onboarding and training costs
3. Open role loss
4. Up-to-speed loss
5. Extra pressure on team leader and members

At first sight, it might seem wise to try and minimise all these costs, but it is worth remembering that the purpose of the recruitment process is to find candidates that are a good fit. Investing soundly in a process that maximises the chances of them fitting the role well and being a good fit for the organisational and team culture is critical. If a process is low-cost but new recruits soon leave, it is a false economy. This is a theme I will return to in Chapter 19 when I estimate the lifetime value of an employee.

For now, let's go through these five costs in turn.

1. Direct recruitment costs

If you use a recruitment agency, they typically charge around 30% of the final salary to create a shortlist of candidates. Even if you manage the process in-house, the time spent on job ads, screening and interviews means the real cost is similar.

When you also factor in internal project management and interview time, a reasonable overall estimate is that recruitment costs amount to around 40% of the final salary.

2. Onboarding and training

Costs here vary by role and company, but onboarding always includes time spent on inductions, covering everything from health and safety to HR policies and IT systems, as well as role-specific training. Let's assume the new hire requires ten days of onboarding. If we estimate the cost of each training day at twice the employee's day rate (to include trainers and setup), that brings us to the equivalent of one month's salary.

3. Cost of the role being vacant

When someone leaves, they usually give at least a month's notice, during which their productivity often drops. It typically takes another month to find and appoint their replacement. During that time, the business incurs costs from lost productivity and may need temporary cover. A fair estimate here is two months' salary.

4. Time to get up-to-speed

It takes time for new hires to become fully effective. While it can take up to a year, a conservative estimate is six months, with a gradual ramp-up. If we assume the new hire is operating at half-capacity during that period, the effective cost is three months' salary. To stay cautious, though, we'll estimate this as two months' salary.

5. Extra pressure on team leaders and members

This is harder to put a number on, but it matters. When someone leaves, managers take on extra work running recruitment and onboarding – tasks that rarely have time budgeted. Colleagues pick up the slack and may find themselves informally training or mentoring the new recruit. If morale dips or burnout sets in, one person leaving can trigger others to follow. While we won't estimate a financial cost here, the ripple effect on team happiness and stability should not be overlooked.

Other costs

In some roles there will be other costs like the need to relocate or the purchase of new equipment. In others there might be risks such as the loss of specialist knowledge or key clients. Whatever the role, it's worth taking the time to consider these costs, as they are often more significant than we first assume.

Cashing out the costs

Now I am going to estimate these costs for a 200-person company, with an average annual salary of £50,000 and staff turnover of 20%.[13] I have used

---

13 The average-sized UK company – where the 'median' employee works – has about 175 employees. In other words, about half of the UK working population works in smaller and half in bigger organisations. In the US the average company employs a slightly higher number, at about 230 people. Average annual salary in the UK is at about £30,000, though full costs of employment are higher. In the US the figure is more like $55,000 per annum. Staff turnover is approximately 20% for both, representing an average tenure of five years.

round numbers so that you can easily rejig them for your organisation.

Costs of staff turnover (estimate)

	Estimate (% of annual salary)	Per role (£50,000 salary)	Cost of 40 hires (per year)
Recruitment costs	40%	£20,000	£800,000
Onboarding/training	8.3%	£4,167	£166,667
Open role loss	16.7%	£8,334	£333,333
Up-to-speed loss	16.7%	£8,334	£333,333
Full cost of new role(s)	81.7%	£40,835	£1,633,333

The numbers speak for themselves, showing that staff turnover comes at a significant cost – for a typical 200-person organisation in excess of £1.5 million.

Happiness reduces staff turnover

It is obvious that unhappy employees are more likely to leave, and even OK employees are 40–50% more likely to. Improving team happiness will reduce staff turnover. It won't completely eliminate it, and that probably wouldn't be healthy anyway, but it is very achievable to reduce it by a quarter, from say 20% to 15% per annum. In the worked example above that would save more than £400,000 every year.

Many of the clients I've worked with have successfully reduced staff turnover. One organisation, with 2,000 employees, has lowered its turnover from 19.9% to 17.1% since the end of the pandemic. Another, with 250 employees, brought it down from 14.5% pre-Covid to just 9.5%. These results are based on comparing figures from 2018/19 to 2022/23. In both cases the reductions not only boosted business profitability but also made the organisations better places to work, with all the added benefits that brings.

Summary

- **Happiness at work reduces staff turnover.** Happier employees are far less likely to leave. Even those who say work is just OK are 40–50% more likely to be looking elsewhere.

- **It's important to count the cost.** Replacing a single leaver can cost more than 80% of their annual salary, presenting a substantial and often underestimated financial burden.

- **We need to invest in happiness.** Happiness is a signal of good fit – between people, their roles and the team culture. To get the best return on recruitment, organisations need to invest in team happiness as a way of sustaining that fit and retaining the talent they've worked hard to find.

13
How The British Weather Helped Prove The Power Of Happiness

In Britain, as everyone knows, we have a lot of grey, cloudy days. Over a year we have roughly half the sunshine of our Southern European cousins. Even within the UK there is a lot of variation, with Cornwall in the southwest of England having 30% more sunny days than Scotland. When the sun does shine, it's consequently a bit of an event for us. It lifts everyone's mood, and of course, being Brits, we reinforce this effect by talking about the weather a lot of the time!

Rather wonderfully, this impact of the weather on our moods has been used in an innovative way to prove that happiness increases productivity. I use the word *prove* carefully here. Most evidence on the link between happiness and productivity is correlational, and as you will have probably heard many times over, correlation doesn't prove causality.

The best study on happiness and productivity

This landmark study was published only recently, in 2023. It involved tracking the weekly happiness and sales of more than 1,750 sales agents at British Telecoms (BT), the UK's largest provider of phone and internet services. It was led by Professor Jan-Emmanuel de Neve from Oxford University, and the resulting paper was titled 'Does employee happiness have an impact on productivity?' (Bellet, De Neve and Ward, 2023). It's a rhetorical question – the answer is a resounding yes. Even more impressive was the clarity of the researchers' methodology, which identified the steps in the process.

The first important thing to note is that, although they all worked for the same business, the sales agents were based in eleven different call centres spread across the UK. The researchers asked the agents every week for six months how happy they were, plus they tracked the numbers and types of sales they made. In this way they could examine the direct impact of weekly mood on people's work performance.

As in almost every other study on workplace happiness, they found that happier operators sold more – in this case 13% more, which is actually a much smaller effect than many other studies. It is important to note, though, that this study was only able to calculate a precise figure for the positive impact of happiness, as all the call operators did a similar role with the same business outcome measure. The interaction between call operators was minimal, as they worked almost completely alone, answering calls routed automatically to them and speaking to any prospective customer only once. These limitations make for a great study, but they also greatly limit the potential ways the operators' moods can impact business outcomes.

The challenge of creating robust measures of productivity is more complex in most organisational settings and even more so across whole economies with multiple sectors. This is why large academic studies tend to report correlation coefficients (betas) to measure the strength of the relationship rather than easier-to-understand percentage changes. One major meta-analysis used data from over 230,000 employees working in 5,800 work units (teams) across multiple sectors. They found that there was a consistent relationship between business unit performance and job satisfaction, though the betas varied between sectors (0.28–0.43), with an average of 0.34 (Whitman et al, 2010).

This is robust evidence that happier teams are more successful, though it is undeniable that correlation coefficients aren't very easy to relate to. I used them earlier, in Chapter 4, to show that boredom was four times worse for happiness than stress. In that instance, though, the three variables – happiness, stress and boredom – were measured in the same survey, using the same five-point response scale, making them easier to compare. I can, however, use my data from clients to estimate that typically a happy team will be between 20% and 30% more productive than an unhappy one.[14] I can also show that unhappy teams are over three times more likely to miss their targets than happier ones. Happier employees and happier teams definitely perform better.

Changes in the weather prove the causal link

The BT study finding alone is not proof of causality, as it is quite possible that operators might have been happier because they sold more. This is where the vagaries of the British weather come into play. By looking at weather reports, the researchers were able to create a *visual weather index* for each call centre, basically rating their weekly weather, from gloomy to sunny. They

---

14 This is estimated using the beta coefficients from this meta-analysis, together with data tracking happiness across 1,000 teams in 2023/4. My precise estimate is that happy teams are 28% more productive than unhappy teams. Some estimates are higher than this, for example 31% (Achor, 2010); and others are lower, for example 21% (Gallup, 2013). Given that there is a lot of variation between sectors, it is best to use a range for the estimate of the impact of happiness on productivity. For a recent academic overview of that relationship, see *Why Workplace Wellbeing Matters* (De Neve and Ward, 2025).

even included the fact that some call centres had lots of windows and others had none.

It was found that in sunnier weeks the call operators felt sunnier themselves and their increased positivity led to more sales. Effectively, the researchers proved a real-world causal pathway: *visible weather changes lead to mood changes, which in turn lead to changes in sales.*

The great thing is that this causal pathway can only flow one way. While it is perfectly possible that sales impact people's moods, there is no way that moods can impact the weather. There is, though, just one other possibility: good weather impacts customers' mood and makes them want to buy more. To rule out this possibility, the researchers showed that because customer calls were routed to the next available operator, regardless of location, they could separate out the impact of national and local weather. In this way they proved that changes in sales were driven not by the customers but by the local weather and its impact on the operators' moods.

This is a groundbreaking piece of research that proves, beyond doubt, that changes in happiness levels impact performance. Of course, relying on something as unpredictable as the weather to boost productivity isn't exactly a strategy. It's far better to build a strong culture where teams are both happy and successful, which, naturally, I'll explore later in the book.

Summary

- **Happiness drives productivity.** A landmark study of 1,750 BT sales agents found that happier employees made 13% more sales, adding hard data to what many of us already sense.

- **The weather made the case.** Researchers proved causality by linking local sunshine levels to improved mood and increased performance, showing that changes in happiness directly influence output.

- **It's time to invest.** The takeaway for organisations is that relying on sunny weather isn't a strategy; investing in workplace happiness is. Happier teams consistently perform better and are less likely to miss targets.

14
Difficult Customers And Complex Deals

The BT study mentioned in Chapter 13 (Bellet, De Neve and Ward, 2023) conclusively proved that feeling happier led to call operators selling more. That still begs the question: Why? What is it about feeling more positive that enables people to do better work?

Barbara Fredrickson's broaden-and-build theory of positive emotions offers some insights (Fredrickson, 2010). Her research suggests that feeling good helps improve creativity and decision-making and enables people to adapt to the situation better. As she puts it, positive emotions 'broaden our repertoire of responses'. However, most of her research is lab-based. How does this play out in a work context, and do we have evidence of it happening?

Why do happy call operators sell more?

As if proving causality wasn't enough, the BT study had a second element to it, which addresses precisely this question. When I introduced the study in the last chapter I said that the researchers measured both the number, *and types*, of sales. Looking at the different types of call enabled the researchers to dig into why the operators sold more, leading to a world of difficult customers and complex deals.

By looking at the different types of calls the operators had to take, the researchers were able to define three categories:

1. Routine order taking for phone lines and internet connections

2. More complicated TV and mobile phone contracts

3. Upgrades and recontracting, which require negotiation, often with disgruntled customers[15]

When they looked at the regression coefficients, happiness had absolutely no effect on the routine order-taking calls. The customers purely wanted the operator to take a simple order, and the mood of

---

15 Data from Table S18 in 'Does employee happiness have an impact on productivity?' (Bellet, De Neve and Ward, 2023). The authors say their results are suggestive rather than definitive; however, they align with other studies such as Fredrickson's lab-based work.

the operator had no impact on the sale. However, the more complex the call, the bigger the impact of the call operator's mood. This was particularly clear when it came to the more complex deals and difficult customers in the third category.

Positivity helps us deal with complexity

Effectively, the operators in a more positive mood could:

- Go off script (literally)
- Better understand the customer's point of view
- De-escalate situations
- Problem solve with customers
- Find a solution (make a sale)

We can all recognise this effect within ourselves. When we are in a bad mood, our attention is on our own inner world, and we are much more likely to get cross with other people. In contrast, when we are in a good mood, we interact with others in a more harmonious way.

The BT study was observational, meaning the researchers didn't intervene – they simply tracked what was already happening, which makes the results especially clean and natural. Outside of the research field, though, progressive business leaders have long recognised the link between happiness and performance. The late Tony Hsieh, former CEO of Zappos (the US online shoe and clothing retailer), was ahead of his time. He was a strong advocate for employee happiness and wrote the best-selling book *Delivering Happiness* to explain his story and philosophy (Hsieh, 2010).

Tony Hsieh's advice for customer calls

I worked with Tony on and off in the early 2010s. Showing me around the Zappos offices in Las Vegas, he told me they didn't have any hard and fast rules for how employees should interact with customers, and certainly no scripts. Employees were encouraged to use their social skills, or as he put it, to 'be themselves' and 'use their judgement'. There were no targets on the length of calls; he used to joke about how the longest one lasted for over ten hours.

As we were walking around, I pushed him a little on his no-rules idea, and it emerged that while there weren't rules, there were strongly encouraged tips, one of which I thought was ingenious. He said that operators were encouraged to make at least two attempts in a call to make an emotional connection with the customer. He gave an example: If the operator heard a dog barking and they loved dogs, they were encouraged to say so – a great way to build a bit of rapport. Another example was that if the caller was from a city the operator knew, they should have a chat about it.

This not only created much more enjoyable calls for the operators but also built a better relationship with the customer. No doubt this was why many customers became passionate advocates for Zappos, and customer relationships became a key part of their strategy for word-of-mouth marketing – the topic of my next chapter.

Zappos' rise was stellar, growing to a billion-dollar business within a decade. Tony Hsieh recognised that employee happiness helps build great relationships both within the business and with customers. The BT study provides statistical evidence to support this link, with the happier call operators being better able to build positive relationships with their customers, leading to more sales. Together, these findings show not only that we can make better connections when we feel good, but that this leads to successful business outcomes too.

Summary

- **Positivity supports complex work.** The BT study showed that happiness had little impact on simple tasks but significantly boosted performance in complex calls involving difficult customers and negotiations.

- **Happy employees build better relationships.** Positive emotions helped operators go off script, empathise, de-escalate and find creative solutions, proving that emotions matter most when situations are challenging.

- **Zappos shows happiness in action.** Tony Hsieh's approach encouraged emotional connection and authentic interaction, turning employee happiness into a competitive advantage through exceptional customer service.

15
How Happiness Lowers The Cost Of Sales

Zappos very intentionally championed employee happiness, with the full expectation that it would increase customer happiness and improve sales. When I was talking with Tony Hsieh, he explained that Zappos had never done any advertising. His logic was that advertisers sought to reach potential customers, but his call operators already spoke directly to customers, so why pay someone else? I am not sure where Tony got his enthusiasm from, but one popular model of the power of customer service is the *service-profit chain*, a concept first introduced in the 1990s by three Harvard Business School researchers (Heskett, Sasser and Schlesinger, 1997).

Below is my version of this model, driven by employee happiness. You can see the impact spreading out from the top left of the diagram and impacting the business's bottom line through three pathways. While this model is relevant to all sorts of businesses, it is especially relevant to high-contact service businesses, including hospitality, retail, and other service-based sectors such as financial services, agencies and consultancies.

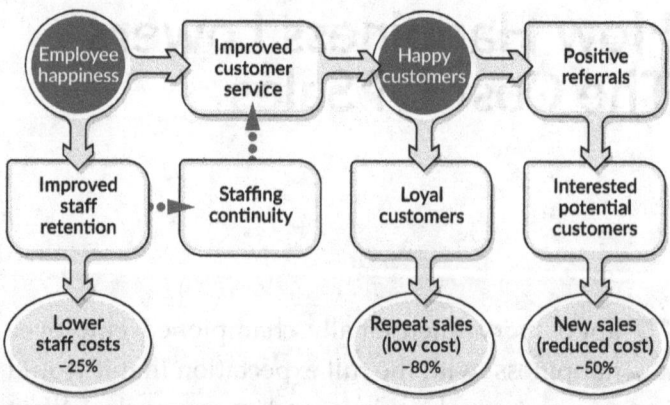

Employee happiness and the customer-service-profit chain (Source: Adapted from Heskett, Sasser and Schlesinger (1997); figures are my estimates of cost reduction)

Happiness and the customer-service-profit chain

There are three main pathways from employee happiness to business success:

1. **Lower staffing costs:** I cashed out the lower costs due to improved retention rates in Chapter 12.

However, notice that stability of staffing has a potential additional impact on customer service, as customers often create a personal relationship with employees. This can be as simple as liking the same receptionist at a hotel to trusting a particular financial services adviser. Stability of staffing creates familiarity, leading to enhanced customer happiness with all its positive knock-on effects.

2. **Repeat sales:** Happy customers are repeat buyers, and retaining customers is often the key to increased profitability. Fredrick Reichheld, the creator of the famous customer satisfaction metric NPS (net promotor score) estimates that the cost of acquiring a new (cold) sale is between five and twenty-five times higher than that of a repeat, warm sale (Reichheld, 2001).

3. **Recommended sales:** Happy customers do your marketing for you by making positive referrals. Referred new customers typically cost 25–50% less than new customers acquired through more traditional marketing channels. This is because they have lower acquisition costs, better conversion rates and higher lifetime value (Trusov, Bucklin and Pauwels 2009).

Customer interactions drive profits

If employees are positive and helpful in their interactions with customers, everything becomes much more pleasant, but does it really power this customer-service-profit chain? The answer is that it does, probably through three ways:

1. **Emotional contagion** – the employee's positive mood rubs off on the customer, creating a more pleasant interaction.

2. **Feelings as information** – customers pick up on how employees are feeling and use that as a cue to judge the trustworthiness or quality of the experience, which can influence their decision to buy.

3. **Enhanced skills** – being in a good mood boosts employees' social and negotiation skills, which is especially helpful in complex or sensitive situations.

As always, there are different effect sizes depending on the context. The impact is smaller, for example, in simple, one-off sales, even though being served by someone positive always makes the customer feel better. In more complex situations with repeated interactions, the effects are considerably larger.

One study of a car hire company with multiple outlets was able to identify an interesting nuance to these effects (Wolter et al, 2019). The researchers measured the happiness of employees at each site and how often customers returned to hire a car from them again. Over time the customers' repeat purchases had less to do with the general mood of the employees, to which the customers had effectively become acclimatised. However, if the mood at the site changed – positively or negatively – that did have an impact on sales. In practice this means that it is never too late to make improvements to team happiness. Customers will notice, and it will make a positive difference. Conversely, once you have achieved a good level of team happiness, make sure you maintain it, as again they will notice the drop and interpret it negatively.

Summary

- **Happier staff lower recruitment costs.** When employees are happier, they stay longer. This reduces recruitment and training costs, and strengthens customer relationships through greater consistency and familiarity.

- **Happy customers are cheaper to sell to.** It costs far less to retain existing customers than to acquire new ones. Happy employees create experiences that encourage loyalty, leading to more repeat and recommended sales.

- **Positivity is contagious (and persuasive).** Positive moods have ripple effects. Happier staff influence customer moods, build trust, and boost sales without needing a script.

16
The Magnetic Attraction Of Happiness

Think about how a magnet powerfully attracts metals towards it. Happiness at work acts in a similar way, drawing in people and creating opportunities. This is particularly true in the recruitment process, whose whole aim is to find candidates who will be a good fit. A workplace culture that people are eager to join and contribute to is a massive advantage. It will not only attract more applications from high-quality candidates but also help them thrive once they start – a powerful combination.

Ultimately, the outcome everyone wants from the process is the new hire being happy in their role – happiness signals they are a good fit. The challenge comes during the process itself, when both sides are trying to predict if the fit will be good.

One issue is that both candidates and organisations often use the wrong criteria when assessing fit. Employers can focus too much on qualifications or technical skills, while jobseekers often prioritise pay, hours and location. It's understandable as all those aspects are tangible and easy to identify. However, it's often the intangibles such as team morale, work–life balance and opportunity to progress that really matter.[16] They are also harder for both sides, especially the candidates, to evaluate, and as a result are frequently overlooked.

For some years now jobseekers have been able to look for clues on websites such as Glassdoor, where current and former employees can leave reviews. These do certainly give some useful insights, but like all social-proof websites, they are subject to biases and even sometimes manipulation.

Collecting happiness at work data

One of the world's largest job sites, Indeed, recently started to invite people to carry out a happiness at work survey (Indeed Editorial Team, 2022). The purpose is to systematically gather data on employees' real experience of work. By the end of 2024 they had collected more than 15 million responses.

---

16 See for example the global BCG survey of over 80,000 people, 'What Job Seekers Wish Employers Knew' (Baier et al, 2023).

Next, in a bold move, they started to experiment with publishing happiness data on organisations' profile pages. The experiment has been led by the well-respected happiness researcher Dr George Ward from MIT (the Massachusetts Institute of Technology). In a clever experiment, he set up some classic A/B tests so that some people could see the company information page with its happiness scores, while other candidates couldn't see that information (Ward, 2023).

Unsurprisingly, Ward found that low happiness scores deterred people from applying, and higher ones encouraged applications. The effect was, however, significantly larger for the low scores. He commented:

> 'Job seekers appear to use the happiness score information to screen out miserable workplaces from their consideration. This accords with a long line of research in psychology that shows that bad is stronger than good.'

What's great about this research is that it is based on real behaviour of real people actively looking for a new role. It shows clearly that happier organisations act like a magnet attracting talent. Of course advertising on job sites isn't the only way that organisations try to fill vacant roles. There is also strong evidence of this attraction effect in other channels such as employee recommendations and internal candidates, both of which are directly influenced by employee happiness.

Recommendations from employees

The mechanism is somewhat similar to the customer-service-profit chain. If employees are happy, they are more likely to recommend the company as a good place to work. This will enable the organisation to attract higher-quality candidates at lower costs.

Recommendations are naturally dependent on employees' goodwill towards the organisation. Unsurprisingly, this is affected by how happy they are or were in their roles. This effect is often measured by a metric – the employee net promoter score (eNPS) – that has been adapted from the marketing NPS. It uses a question like this: How likely is it that you would recommend this organisation to a friend as a good place to work?

Respondents typically answer on a scale of 0 to 10. If they score 9 or 10, they are called *promoters*, while those who score 6 or below are called *detractors*. Some organisations use this score as a proxy measure of employee happiness, which I must admit to not being keen on, as it exclusively reflects the organisation's agenda rather than that of the employee. That being said, happiness and eNPS are highly correlated. I have created the graph below using data from one of the many representative surveys I have conducted over the years. This specific graph comes from a representative sample of 1,598 UK workers in 2011.

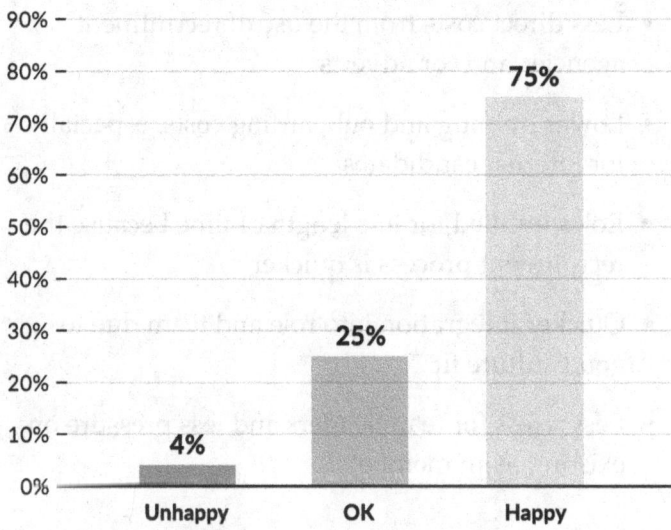

Percentage within each happiness group who would recommend their employer as a good place to work

This graph provides strong evidence that happy employees are much more likely to communicate their positive feelings about their organisation to the outside world. The happy employees were more than three times more likely to recommend their organisation as a great place to work than those who merely felt OK. The unhappy rarely do; in fact, the same data showed that more than 70% of them were detractors, pushing people away.

Just as happy employees reduce sales costs, as shown by the customer-service-profit chain, they also help bring down recruitment costs, especially in the ways I outlined in Chapter 12:

- Less direct costs from the use of recruitment agencies and/or adverts

- Lower training and onboarding costs, especially for internal candidates

- Roles unfilled for less length of time because the recruitment process is quicker

- Quicker integration into role and team due to good culture fit

- Less stress for team leaders and less pressure on existing team members

Summary

- **Happiness attracts talent.** Just like a magnet, a happy workplace draws in great people, especially those looking for a good fit. A positive culture isn't just nice to have; it's also a competitive edge in recruitment.

- **Jobseekers are watching.** Platforms like Indeed and Glassdoor mean workplace culture is increasingly transparent. People are more likely to apply to happier organisations and avoid those with low scores.

- **Happy employees spread the word.** When people enjoy where they work, they recommend it. This boosts internal referrals, speeds up recruitment and lowers costs – another way happiness pays dividends.

17
Everyday Creativity And Happiness

We all know about tortured souls suffering for their art. The list is long, from Vincent van Gogh to Robin Williams, Sylvia Plath to Amy Winehouse – all geniuses in their artistic fields. Creativity is not just the preserve of artists, though – we all need to be creative in our everyday lives, especially at work. An EU survey (Vermeylen et al, 2012) found that more than 80% of jobs require some creativity, such as solving unforeseen problems or applying original ideas. Crucially, creativity is the precursor to innovation. That's why the phrase *innovate or die* has become such a mantra in today's business world; it captures the vital role creativity plays in driving progress and staying competitive.

The image of the tortured artist – the idea that great ideas arise from pain and suffering – continues to haunt our ideas about creativity. It is simply not true, though, that the everyday creativity needed at work is facilitated by negative emotions. Indeed, it is quite the opposite. As Barbara Fredrickson's broaden-and-build theory highlights, positive emotions amplify our ability to respond to challenges. We solve problems better and come up with more new ideas when we are happy.

Feeling positive improves problem-solving

There is a famous experiment in psychological research that nicely illustrates this. It was invented in the 1930s by Karl Duncker, a German psychologist who was himself a bit of a tortured genius. Despite emigrating to the US to escape Nazism, he couldn't escape his own demons, and sadly, after a long bout of depression in 1940, he took his own life (Seel, 2012). His insights live on, though, especially in a particular creative problem-solving task he designed, which has become known as the Duncker candle problem. These are typical instructions for it:

> On the table are a book of matches, a box of tacks and a candle. Above the table on the wall is a corkboard. Your task is to affix the candle

to the corkboard in such a way that it will burn without dripping wax onto the table or the floor beneath. You will be given ten minutes to work on the problem.

It's a bit of a mind mess until you recognise the solution – that you have a box as well as some tacks. The puzzle was designed to create insights into problem-solving strategies, which of course require creativity.

In the 1980s another psychologist, Alice Isen, used it in a novel way to test whether positive emotions facilitated creative problem-solving. In a series of lab-based experiments she randomly assigned people into positive and neutral mood groups. She used various ways, including showing comedy video clips or giving candy bars to those in the positive mood group. Meanwhile, those in the neutral groups got to watch a maths video about measuring the area under a graph – something surely only a statistician like me would love!

The results were clear, with those in a positive mood much more likely to solve the problem.

It is interesting that the comedy video had a much larger impact than the candy bar. Certainly, receiving a candy bar as a gift will feel nice at the time, but it is a much more passive form of positivity than laughing at a film.[17] Laughter is typically a social behaviour that helps us connect with other people, so although Isen's test was conducted in a lab setting, it suggests that there is a social side to creativity too.

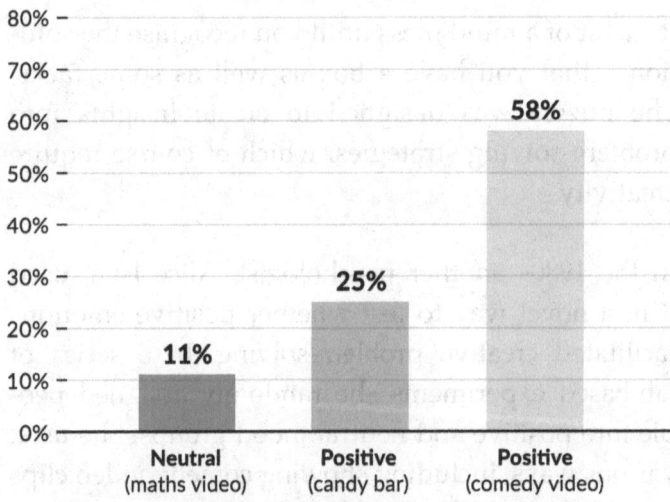

Mood and problem-solving – percentage within each group able to solve the Duncker candle problem (Source: Isen, Daubman and Nowicki (1987))

Teresa Amabile, whose work I referred to in Chapter 7 on friction and flow, is a globally renowned expert on creativity. In her book, *The Progress Principle* (Amabile and Kramer, 2011), she reflects on Isen's classic piece of research: 'Because of the random assignment

---

17 This makes me wonder whether 'gifting' schemes – someone making a gift to a colleague – are valuable. They do, though, often have a social element attached to them; publicly thanking someone definitely builds happiness and stronger bonds.

and careful laboratory control of the situation, this experiment – like others by Isen – demonstrates cause and effect: positive emotion leads to better creative problem-solving.'

Feeling good today boosts creativity tomorrow

Professor Amabile also explored the link between people's mood and creativity in her large diary study, in which people filled in a diary at the end of every workday. They outlined what they had done that day as well as recording their mood, which made it possible to identify whether the participants had used creative thinking that day. One interesting thing about this research is that it simply observed what people did in their everyday work is precisely the type of creativity that businesses need on a day-to-day basis. In one research paper Amabile cites some great examples of people reflecting on their day, including one from an engineer:

> 'In consideration of the enormous complexity and machinery involvement, I was forced to think. An alternative idea soon came to mind. This not only simplifies our trial tremendously, it also vastly increases the probability of success ... It saves about six man days of labor, a week of schedule time, and over a thousand

dollars in outside cleaning costs. This win-win eureka boosted our spirits and let us finish the week on a high note.' (Amabile et al, 2005)

It is clear this engineer was not only being creative but also enjoying it, creativity and positive emotions going hand in hand. That's great, but it does create a statistical challenge – it's not immediately clear whether positive mood is driving creativity or the other way round. While initial analyses did show that instances of creativity were significantly more likely on days of positive emotion the causality wasn't proven. However, as diary entries were collected from consecutive days, the interaction between creativity and mood over time could be explored. This way the causality was clear:

- If someone was in a positive mood one day, they were more likely to be creative on the next day (and even the day after that).
- If they were creative on the first day, however, there was no increased likelihood of being happier the next.

This is an important finding, as it shows the causal link from positivity to creativity. It also seems to provide evidence of a slightly mysterious phenomenon that we are all aware of: if we sleep on a problem, we often wake with a fresh idea about how to solve it. Quite possibly, this highly productive unconscious process is also aided by us feeling good. That makes intuitive sense, as nightmares clearly arise out of psychological dis-ease, so why shouldn't the opposite be true, that positive imaginations arise out of psychological ease?

What is clear is that you don't have to be a tortured artist to be creative. Everyday creativity is fuelled by feeling positive, and it is precisely this type of creativity that businesses need to power their innovation.

Summary

- **Positivity unlocks problem-solving.** Experiments show that people in a good mood are more likely to solve creative challenges – like the famous candle problem – because positive emotions help us think more flexibly and spot unusual solutions.

- **Feeling good today fuels tomorrow's ideas.** Diary research by Teresa Amabile revealed that people in a positive mood one day are more likely to be creative the next – even two days later – confirming that happiness leads, rather than follows, creativity.

- **Everyday creativity powers innovation.** You don't have to suffer for your art – feeling good helps generate fresh ideas in everyday work. From engineers to team leaders, positive emotions boost the kind of creative thinking that drives progress.

18
Fired Up Or Burnt Out?

Sometimes burnout can creep up on us. We can be fired up about a project, and then slowly over time, we start to feel we are running on empty. At other times burnout just hits people, and they collapse. That has thankfully never happened to me, but there have definitely been times when work has left me feeling totally drained.

Due in part to the wide range of causes and experience, there is also a broad array of estimates for the number of people who suffer from burnout. Even the World Health Organization definition (WHO, 2019) leaves a lot of room for interpretation of severity:

> 'Burn-out is a syndrome conceptualized as resulting from chronic workplace stress that

has not been successfully managed. It is characterized by three dimensions:

- feelings of energy depletion or exhaustion;
- increased mental distance from one's job, or feelings of negativism or cynicism related to one's job; and
- reduced professional efficacy.'

Feeling burnout is all too common

In one particularly robust study of US health practitioners, the authors found that their estimates of burnout could range dramatically – from just 3% to as high as 91% – depending entirely on how they defined burnout. At the low end, the figure reflected only those who experienced all three WHO-defined symptoms daily. At the high end, it included anyone who reported at least one symptom a few times a year. This wide spread shows how crucial the definition is. Still, their mid-range estimates figures were striking: 39% of health workers reported feeling emotionally exhausted every week, and over 70% said they experienced it at least once a month (Hewitt et al, 2020).

These are depressing statistics for a sector whose whole purpose is caring about people's health. Health practitioners also sometimes suffer from what some researchers call *compassion fatigue*, where continued exposure to the suffering of others leads to a reduced capacity to empathise. This is illustrated, for example, in the report 'Compassion Fatigue among Healthcare, Emergency and Community Service Workers' (Cocker and Joss, 2016). The findings around compassion fatigue are backed up by multiple sources, which show that the sectors with the highest rates of burnout are healthcare, education and hospitality.[18]

The pace of work is increasing

Burnout is certainly gaining wider recognition as an issue, but that might mean only that it is more talked about, not necessarily that it is becoming more prevalent. To understand if case numbers are on the increase, consistent time-series data is needed, with that data being rare. It's not entirely absent, though – the British Skills and Employment Survey (SES), conducted about every five years, includes a series of questions about work intensity. In 2021 Professor Francis Green, who has been instrumental in the design of the SES, published a paper called 'Working Still Harder' (Green et al, 2021), which showed that people are working at a higher speed and to tighter deadlines.

---

18 I find this in my data, including a representative sample of the UK working population in January 2023. Other public data also shows this, for example that in 'Industries with the highest employee burnout rate worldwide in 2019' (Dyvik, 2024).

The graph below shows the trends as well as a *high work intensity index* included in Green's report.

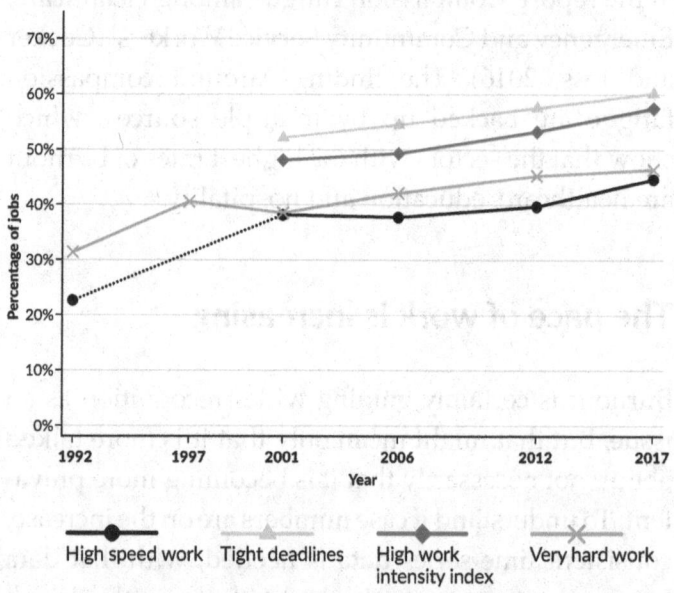

Trends in work intensity in Britain, 1992–2017

This graph shows that work intensity has increased by about 10% since the early 2000s. This might sound like a positive – that workers are being 10% more productive – but this hasn't been the case at all, with UK productivity gains being notoriously flat since the financial crisis of 2008 (Samiri and Millard, 2022). Instead, feeling over-pressured is more about not feeling in control of our work.

While work intensity isn't identical to burnout, it is a key risk factor for it. Another research paper, based on the same SES data, showed that people who worked in high-intensity jobs were, at the end of their working days, much more likely to feel 'used up' and found it 'difficult to unwind' (Hunt and Pickard, 2022). Those feelings are both red flags for burnout and depression.

Happiness protects against burnout

Burnout is most certainly a serious issue. As the WHO definition above points out, good management can also make burnout avoidable. In my data I see strong support for this, as happier employees are much less likely to get burnt out. I use one relatively simple question about burnout rather than a full diagnostic, but the results identify that about 45% of people have had mild to moderate burnout in the last year, and 15% have experienced severe burnout. These figures align quite well with the much more in-depth US healthcare study (Hewitt et al, 2020).[19]

The graph below shows the relationship between burnout and employee happiness.

---

[19] I introduce burnout carefully in my surveys, as there are many interpretations of the word. This is the preamble to my question: 'Burnout is defined as when someone is emotionally exhausted, with their work efficiency suffering, due to too much involvement in their work.' I then ask the employees if they have experienced it in the last year. The US healthcare study (Hewitt et al, 2020) used six questions. A full diagnostic might use as many as thirty to forty questions.

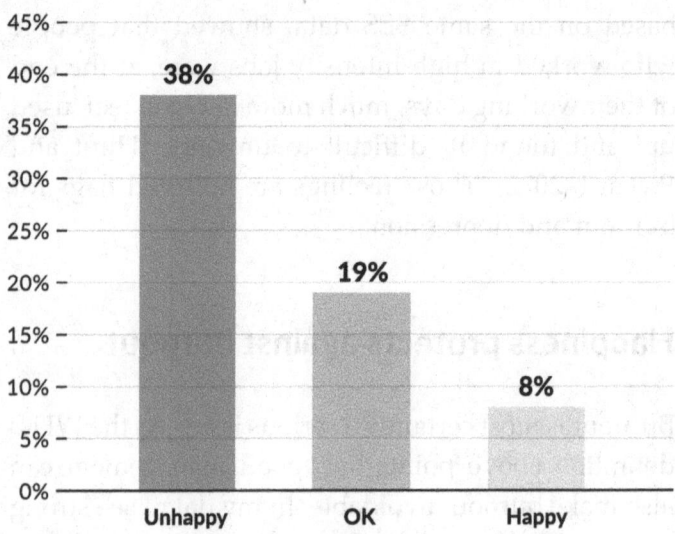

Burnout and employee happiness – percentage within each group experiencing severe burnout

There's a strong link between unhappiness and burnout – those who are unhappy at work are much more likely to burn out. Since this is correlational data, though, it doesn't prove that unhappiness causes burnout – only that the two often go hand in hand. Proving causality is much harder, which is why the BT study discussed in Chapter 13 stands out as such a rare and valuable example.

I'll explore burnout risk factors in more detail later, but it won't surprise anyone to learn that poor work–life balance tops the list. In fact, being seriously out of balance is almost a definition of burnout.

Summary

- **Burnout is common, by any reasonable standard.** Even using reasonable yet serious criteria – like weekly or monthly experiences of emotional exhaustion – studies show that large numbers of workers are feeling the strain. It's a widespread issue that can't be ignored.

- **The pace of work is accelerating.** Data from the British Skills and Employment Survey shows a clear rise in work intensity since the early 2000s. This has not translated into higher productivity, but it has made burnout more likely.

- **Happiness is a buffer against burnout.** Happier employees are much less likely to report feeling burnt out. While correlation doesn't prove causation, this consistent pattern suggests that improving workplace happiness – especially by addressing work–life balance – can help protect people from reaching breaking point.

19
Double Or Quits

This is a key chapter in this book. It will show that happy employees are much more valuable than most people realise.

When I carefully cash out the figures, it shows they are more than twice as valuable than employees that are just OK. This is a bold claim, especially when the evidence I have already shared shows that happier employees are about 20–30% more productive – a sizeable amount but way short of double.

The difference comes from the fact that happier employees also stay longer in an organisation, which means that they add value for a longer period. Effectively, happiness increases both tenure and productivity, and the interaction between tenure and productivity amplifies the impact of happiness. Put this together with the fact that the costs of recruitment are higher than most people realise, then you get towards my 'twice as valuable' claim.

To properly calculate the value employees add, I am going to have to take you through a few steps. There is a nice and clear graph at the end of them, so please stick with me.

The lifetime value of an employee

Sales and marketing teams have long understood the importance of estimating a customer's lifetime value (LTV), not just the value of their first purchase. This thinking is one reason subscription-based models are so successful – customers keep buying over time. Having a reliable LTV estimate also helps sales teams decide how much they can invest in acquiring each new customer.

Business leaders track these kinds of sales metrics obsessively, yet they rarely apply the same logic to hiring and retaining employees. Few organisations consider what we might call eLTV: the *employee lifetime value*.

In the next section, I'll estimate eLTV for three types of employees: one who's happy, one who's just OK and one who's unhappy. For simplicity, I'm assuming each of them stays in the same state throughout. Of course, in real life, people become more or less happy over time, usually in response to their team environment, as we'll explore later. For now, let's treat them as three separate characters.

We have already – in Chapter 12 – estimated the full cost of recruitment at more than 80% of annual salary. Much of that cost comes before employees even start their new job, and then it takes them some time to get up to speed and begin to add value.

Taking all of these factors together gives what is often called *time to value*. Typically, this will be between six and eighteen months, which means that an average new recruit doesn't add any value until their second year of employment. It's quite a sobering analysis. It also highlights just how important the recruitment process is. While often viewed as a cost, it is better understood as an investment – one that delivers a far greater return when the successful candidate is a good fit.

Earlier I shared that happy employees tend to be between 20% and 30% more productive. To stay on the cautious side, I'll use the lower end, 20%. This figure reflects a comparison between happy and unhappy employees. For simplicity, let's assume that employees who feel just OK fall midway – around 10% more productive than unhappy ones and 10% less productive than happy ones.

In practice this means that happy employees will take less *time to value*, so organisations will more quickly recoup their upfront investment in the recruitment process. Using the estimates I have suggested above, this translates into a happy employee (who is also a good fit) taking nine months, an OK one twelve months and an unhappy one seventeen months to start adding value in their new role.[20]

It doesn't end there, though, as unhappy employees who aren't a good fit will leave sooner. Average tenure is about five years for people over twenty-five years of age in the US and the UK, although that varies a lot by both age and sector. As examples: younger people tend to leave jobs more quickly, with the average for under-thirty-five-year-olds being two and a half years. The hospitality sector as a whole has a similar level, while public sector workers and older employees (over forty-five) have an average tenure of more than eight years (Bureau of Labor Statistics, 2024).[21]

In addition to productivity, happiness impacts tenure, with unhappy employees about three times as likely

---

20 While these estimates are approximate, the ratios between them will be consistent as they are all relative to annual salary. The only other factor I have had to estimate is how much value above their salary they add. I have used a figure of one and a half times their annual salary.

21 The UK doesn't have official tenure figures, but data from the 2022 Labour Force Survey publishes tenure bands that suggest the UK is broadly similar to the USA.

to leave than OK employees, and happy employees about 30% less likely to.[22] If we translate these figures into average tenure for happy, OK and unhappy employees, the figures are roughly seven, five and two years, respectively.[23]

The graph below shows how this all fits together.

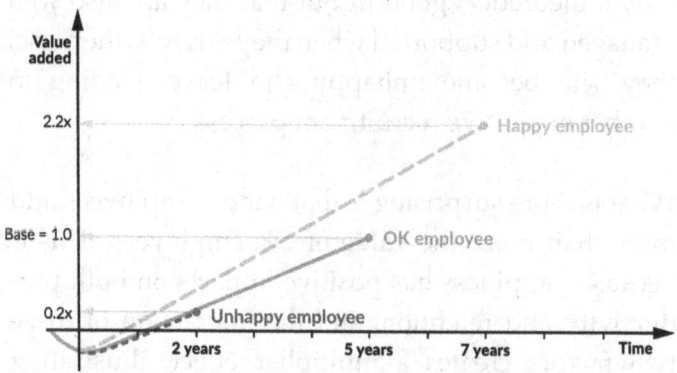

The lifetime value of employees – by happiness level

---

22 I am comparing the happy to the baseline of the OK here, so although the OK are 40–50% more likely to leave than the happy, this is equivalent to the happy being 30% less likely to. 10/7 = 1.42, ie 42% more, whereas 7/10 = 0.7, ie 30% less. Percentages can be confusing!

23 Tenure = 1/{turnover rate}, so a five-year tenure is equivalent to a 20% turnover rate. This aligns well with the data on whether employees intend to quit within the next six months, with the mean being approximately 10%. The precise figures for the happy and unhappy are 7.2 years and 1.8 years, respectively; but as this is an estimation process, I have rounded to the nearest whole year.

The unhappy quit, and the happy add twice as much value as the OK

Perhaps it isn't a huge surprise that the unhappy employee will have added hardly any value before they quit. That fact does serve as a reminder, though, that it is vital to ensure that new employees are not only a theoretical good fit but that they are also well managed and supported when they arrive. Otherwise, they will become unhappy and leave, leading to another expensive recruitment process.

What is more surprising is that happy employees add more than twice the value of OK employees. This is because happiness has positive impacts on both productivity and retention, and the interaction of these two factors creates a multiplier effect, illustrating again that OK isn't OK. Those employees won't be making a fuss, but they won't be making as much positive impact either. They are all too easy to ignore, on the assumption that they aren't doing any harm, but they could clearly be adding a lot more value.

This is literally a case of double or quits – double the performance versus employees leaving. In fact, it would be hard to think of any other single business variable that can predict such a large positive impact. Happiness is not only a serious business; it's also a serious business indicator.

Summary

- **Happier employees stay longer and perform better.** While happiness typically boosts productivity by 20–30%, its full value emerges over time, as happier employees also stay in their roles longer, multiplying their overall contribution.

- **Tracking happiness reveals ongoing fit.** Because hiring is a major investment, organisations get the best return when new recruits are a good fit and stay long enough to make a sustained impact. Tracking happiness provides a continuous indicator of that fit over time.

- **The multiplier effect is real.** Happy employees add more than twice the value of those who are just OK, thanks to the combined impact of greater productivity and longer tenure. It's a compelling case for taking happiness seriously as a business indicator.

20
The Happiness Dividend

I have presented a lot of evidence of happiness leading to success. However, the ultimate evidence would surely be if companies with great cultures were more profitable and had higher share price growth. Increased profits must mean that the benefits of a great culture are significantly larger than the costs of building one.

Naturally, this is a question that researchers have sought to answer. It has been hard, though, to address it statistically, as profits and the movement of stock markets are volatile. In addition, robust information about a company's culture is hard to access. In my statistical opinion, the best paper on this subject, thanks to its passionate attention to detail, was published in 2011 by Alex Edmans (Edmans, 2011), who is now a professor at the London Business School. He has recently published a great book, *May Contain Lies* (Edmans, 2024), in which he explains how biases, misinterpretations and vested interests can lead to the misuse of statistics by politicians, journalists and business consultants, among others.

In his 2011 paper, Edmans effectively tracks the share prices of *Fortune Magazine*'s 'Best 100 Companies to Work For' list, showing that they had a higher share price return than equivalent firms. He also wrote an exceptional executive summary at the start of the paper, which I am going to quote in full, using his own words to avoid introducing any biases:

> 'How are job satisfaction and firm value linked? I tackle this long-standing management question using a new methodology from finance. I study the effect on firm-level value, rather than employee-level productivity, to take into account the cost of increasing job satisfaction. To address reverse causality, I measure firm value by using future stock returns, controlling for risk, firm characteristics, industry performance, and outliers. Companies listed in the '100 Best Companies to Work For in America' generated 2.3% to 3.8% higher stock returns per year than their peers from 1984 through 2011. These results have three main implications. First, consistent with human resource management

theories, job satisfaction is beneficial for firm value. Second, corporate social responsibility can improve stock returns. Third, the stock market does not fully value intangible assets, and so it may be necessary to shield managers from short-term stock prices to encourage long-run growth.'

Share price growth in happier companies

Let's just step back and think about what that means. Personally, I think Warren Buffett would be very happy with 2.3% to 3.8% extra share price growth per year! Over a ten-year period, that is an extra 25–45% return on investment. It's a large effect, but Edmans came to these figures carefully, and they can be directly attributed to a better company culture.[24]

Edmans's classic paper is now over a decade old, so it is reasonable to ask whether this effect continued during the volatile years since. The answer is yes. His result was replicated in 2024 by Professor Jan-Emmanuel de Neve and colleagues from Oxford

---

24 His thorough methodology means that if, say, the Fortune-100 list included lots of tech companies and the tech sector grew faster than other sectors, this wouldn't bias the figures. He also looked at the impact of outliers – single firms that had a disproportionate effect such as, say, Apple. When he removed these outliers, he came to the higher 3.8% figure.

University's Wellbeing Research Centre (De Neve, Kaats and Ward, 2024). Their study is based on the crowdsourced employee happiness and wellbeing data collected by the job site Indeed, as mentioned in Chapter 16, which has amassed more than 15 million responses to its survey since its launch.[25] Indeed created a 'wellbeing index' for each company that had a sufficient number of responses. Through a series of regression analyses the researchers found that 'the wellbeing index proves to be strongly predictive of firm value, return on assets, and profits'.

Ultimately, the Edmans and Indeed research papers demonstrate that building a great culture isn't just nice to have – it unlocks a happiness dividend.

---

25 For a discussion about data quality in these crowdsourced samples, see 'Assessing data quality in a Big convenience sample of work wellbeing' (Fleming, Ward and De Neve, 2024).

Summary

- **Happier companies outperform their peers.** Alex Edmans's landmark 2011 study showed that companies on the 100 Best Companies to Work For list outperformed similar firms by 2.3% to 3.8% in annual share price returns, adding up to a 25–45% advantage over a decade.

- **The culture-profit link is real and replicable.** A 2024 Oxford study using over 15 million data points from Indeed confirmed the link between employee wellbeing and higher profits, return on assets, and firm value.

- **Culture is a competitive advantage.** The happiness dividend isn't just a theory – it's tangible. Investing in workplace happiness creates long-term financial gains, showing that culture is not a cost centre but a growth engine.

PART FOUR
HAPPINESS IS A TEAM SPORT

21
Teams Are Where The Magic Happens

Empirical evidence is important, and while I know that magic doesn't really exist, creating positive change sometimes feels a bit magical. Perhaps it is as much an art as a science. In that spirit, I want to start this section on teams by quoting a poem.

Appropriately, it is by David Whyte, who sometimes describes himself as a corporate poet. This poem, called *Working Together* (Whyte, 2011), was commissioned by Boeing for the launch of its 777 aircraft in 1994.

These are the first few lines:

> We shape our self
> to fit this world
> and by the world
> are shaped again.

> The visible
> and the invisible
> working together
> in common cause,
> to produce
> the miraculous.

For me this is an almost perfect articulation of how teams can come together and produce great work.

The dance between individuals and the system

I love the dance in the opening lines, between us as individuals and the system we are embedded in:

> We shape our self
> to fit the world
> and by the world
> are shaped again.

When we work with others in a team, we are shaped, often unconsciously, by the people around us.

The second couplet builds on this insight:

> The visible
> and the invisible
> working together
> in common cause,
> to produce
> the miraculous.

He is articulating the synergy we have all experienced: in a team, people's energy and ideas build on others', and suddenly the whole is more than the sum of the parts.

Claire Hughes Johnson, COO of the successful tech payments business Stripe, reflects on this point in her book *Scaling People* (Hughes Johnson, 2023): 'It's truly a milestone when the people you manage come together as a team and work as an integrated entity rather than as a set of individuals working alone.' Her language is less poetic, but her insight is borne out of years of practical experience in scaling Stripe from a few hundred to several thousand employees.

Teams working together towards a common cause really can produce the miraculous (or they can at least get the job done). Teams also shape our experience of work, and this applies especially to our happiness at work.

Summary

- **Teams shape us.** We influence the teams we join, and they shape us in return – often in unseen ways.

- **Teams show the magic of synergy.** When people truly work together as a team, ideas build, energy flows and something greater emerges.

- **Teams are where happiness lives.** Our experience of work – and our happiness – depends more on our teams than almost anything else.

22
Great Teams Are Happy And Successful

David Whyte's poem celebrates the power of teams, which are the foundation of every organisation. For most of us, teams are also central to our daily experience of work. When we're in a great team, it's a joy, but when teams are dysfunctional, we have a pretty miserable experience.

Given their importance, I find it strange that the language used to describe great teams is often vague or long-winded. Sometimes people reach for analogies from sports or science, saying that certain teams have a 'winning mindset' or have 'good chemistry'. In contrast, consultants and academics in the field tend to describe great teams by the factors that make them effective, such as their structure, their skills and how the team members develop as a group. One classic definition of a great team is: 'A small number of people with complementary skills who are committed to a common purpose, performance goals, and approach for which they hold themselves mutually accountable.' (Katzenbach and Smith, 1993)

That is a solid definition, but it's quite unwieldy. From a statistical perspective, it is also somewhat circular. Katzenbach and Smith define great teams by the very factors the team members believe make them great, rather than by the team's actual greatness.

I take a different approach. Instead of defining great teams by their drivers, I define them by their outcomes. Hence, my definition is simple: 'A great team is happy and successful.'

This is clear, relatable and appealing. Who would not want to be part of a happy, successful team? Likewise, the opposite is obviously undesirable – no one wants the miserable experience of being part of an unhappy, unsuccessful team.

A simple quadrant of happiness × performance

I use a simple quadrant to visualise the relationship between happiness and performance. Below is a grid where performance runs horizontally from poor to good, and happiness runs vertically from low to high.

GREAT TEAMS ARE HAPPY AND SUCCESSFUL

	Underperforming	Performing well
Happy	SLACKING	GREAT
Not happy	MISERABLE	BURNING OUT

Quadrant of team happiness × performance

At the top right of the quadrant are the great teams, the ones we all want to be in, that are both happy and successful. At the bottom left are the miserable teams, the ones we all want to avoid.

Then there are the other two quadrants. At the top left are teams that are happy but not performing well. I call these *slacking teams*. Many business leaders worry that prioritising team happiness will lead to this outcome, ie people slacking off. It does happen, but data shows that these teams are far less common than those in the bottom right – the *burning-out teams* – those that perform well but are unhappy. While they may seem successful in the short term, they are not sustainable.

Neither slacking or burning-out teams can sustain themselves. Slacking teams consistently miss their targets and risk going out of business; burning-out teams face high turnover as exhausted team members leave the business. The only path to long-term success is to focus on both performance and happiness, ensuring they are aligned and mutually reinforcing.

Over your working life, you have probably found yourself at different times in each of these quadrants. You are likely to know where your current team sits. What is clear is that wherever a team is now, their future will be more secure if it moves towards the top-right quadrant.

Populating the quadrant with data

To bring the quadrant to life statistically, indicators for both team happiness and performance are needed within the same dataset. This was the real strength of the BT study, where researchers had access to weekly mood ratings from call operators alongside their actual sales figures. In contrast, the data I work with – whether from client organisations or wider population surveys – doesn't include such precise performance metrics.

Instead, I use a simpler proxy: asking people how successful their team is at meeting its targets. It's not a gold-standard measure, but it's a useful indicator that allows for a basic categorisation of team performance as high or low. Importantly, it shows a clear relationship with happiness: those who are not happy – including both OK and unhappy responses – are more than four times as likely to report that their team is not meeting its targets than those who are happy.

Using this categorisation, the four graphs below show how people are distributed across the quadrants, along with their likelihood to leave, risk of burnout, and how they rate their manager. All of this data is drawn from my 2023 representative sample of the UK working population.

GREAT TEAMS ARE HAPPY AND SUCCESSFUL

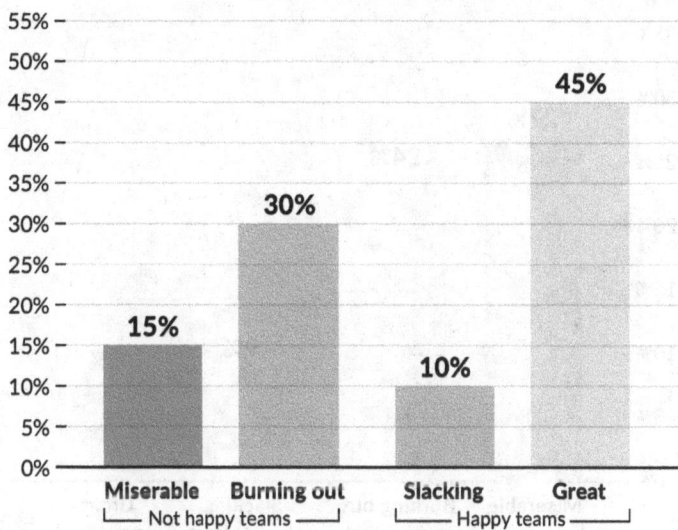

Percentage of teams in each category

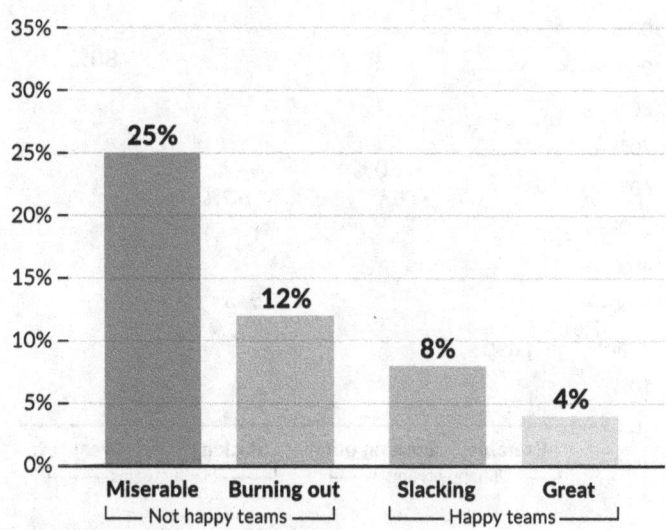

Percentage of employees in each group very likely to leave

HAPPINESS IS A SERIOUS BUSINESS

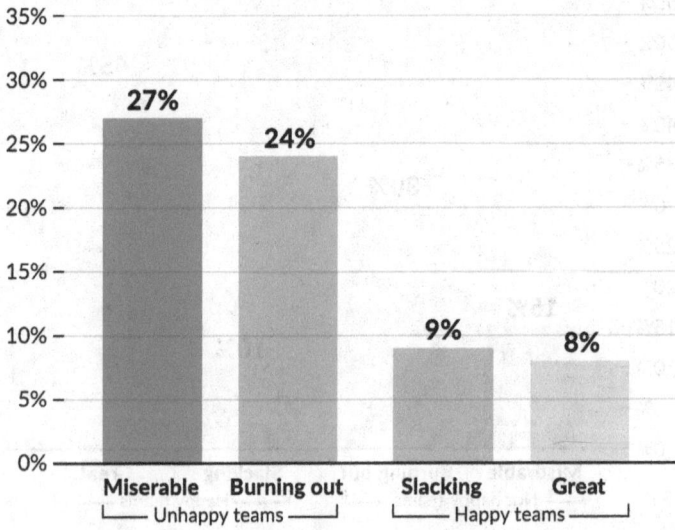

Percentage of employees in each group who felt burnt out

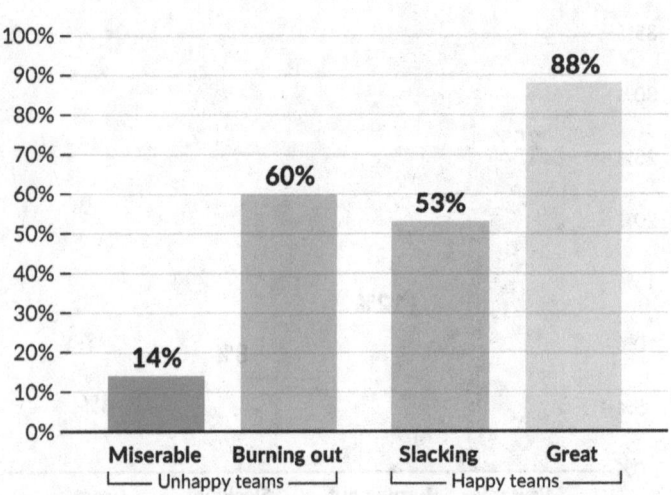

Percentage of employees in each group rating team as well managed

The first graph above shows that most happy teams are also high performing. Happiness and performance generally go hand in hand, though the fact that some people are in slacking teams shows that while happiness tends to improve performance, it does not guarantee it. It's worth noting that burning-out teams are three times more common than slacking ones.

The second graph highlights staff turnover. Employees in the high-performing but unhappy quadrant are more than three times more likely to leave than those in great teams. Given the high cost of recruitment, this makes burning-out teams a significant business risk.

The third graph focuses on burnout rates, showing that burnout is almost entirely driven by unhappiness rather than by performance. Unhappy teams experience three times higher burnout rates. More detailed modelling, which I will share later, suggests that burnout is mainly caused by poor work–life balance and a lack of appreciation. In other words, teams working long hours for extended periods without recognition are at the greatest risk of burnout.

The final graph examines how employees rate their managers. People in great teams rate their managers highly, reinforcing why leading a happy team is so rewarding – your team will value you. Interestingly, despite them feeling happy, employees in slacking teams recognise that they are not well managed.

Together, these insights show why happiness and performance must be considered together, not in isolation. Great teams don't happen by chance – they are built through a conscious effort to create the right conditions for people to thrive and succeed. The quadrant offers a powerful diagnostic lens, helping leaders understand where their teams are now and what risks or opportunities they face. Whether your team is slacking, burning out or already performing well, the goal is the same: move towards the top right. That's where great teams live – ones that are happy, successful and built to last.

Summary

- **Great teams are happy and successful.** The best teams aren't just effective – they feel good to be part of too. When happiness and performance align, everyone thrives.

- **Burning out and slacking teams don't last.** Underperforming but happy teams are relatively rare. Far more common are high-performing but unhappy teams. Neither is sustainable in the long run.

- **Happiness and performance reinforce each other.** Data shows that most top-performing teams are also happy. Great teams don't just succeed, they sustain success.

23
Happiness Starts With The Team

It's obvious that teams matter. You've probably worked in several over the years, and chances are you enjoyed some more than others. Our day-to-day experience at work is shaped hugely by the people we work with and how we're managed.

In my data I've consistently seen the same pattern: even within a single organisation, there are countless team-based microcultures. Some teams are thriving in a mostly unhappy company, while others struggle in an otherwise positive environment.

As someone who likes to put numbers on things, I started wondering: how much do teams really matter? Could I measure it?

The power of the local context

Strangely, the fact that teams shape people's experience of work isn't a point that is often made in research – possibly because it is unusual to have the data to demonstrate that fact. Teresa Amabile certainly noticed it in her in-depth diary study, though her finding is somewhat buried away in her book's appendix (Amabile and Kramer, 2011). She looked at what she called 'the power of the local context' by comparing the different impacts of local team-based culture and the broader organisational culture. She wrote, 'the results were striking ... only the local environment had a significant effect'.

I wanted to know more about Amabile's finding so contacted her while researching this book. She replied: 'I agree that that finding is fascinating, but we never took the time to publish a paper on it (partly because it was, after all, just one set of regressions). Sorry about that.' (Amabile, personal communication, 2025)

She is right to see her results as only indicative, as they are based on 'only one set of regressions'. Her large diary study was insightful because it was such an in-depth study, but it did include only twenty-six teams from seven organisations. Teasing out the different effects of teams and organisations requires data from more teams across more organisations. Luckily, this is precisely what I have in my own data, which tracks the happiness of thousands of teams across hundreds of organisations. This bigger data enables the use of a technique called *multilevel modelling*, where variance is allocated to different levels of the model. Using this technique, I have created the chart below, which shows the percentage of the variation between individuals' happiness that is attributable to their membership of particular teams and organisations.[26]

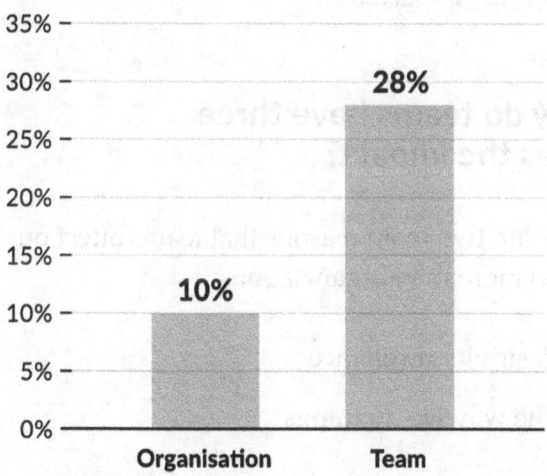

Percentage of happiness explained by team vs organisational culture

---

[26] I used a general linear model (GLM) to look at how much of the variation in employee happiness is explained by team membership versus organisational membership. Teams were treated as nested within organisations, and to get more reliable results, I included only teams that had three or more members. This specific analysis covered more than 10,000 people in over 1,000 teams across 80 organisations. It shows that team culture is about 2.8 times more important than organisational culture for employee happiness. The finding was stable across all four quarters in 2023. As a point of interest I also found that team culture was 2.2x more important for explaining team performance.

The bar chart shows that while organisations do have an impact, they account for only 10% of the variance in people's happiness at work. In contrast, the team we work in explains 28% – nearly three times as much. This analysis puts a clear number on something many of us intuitively feel: teams play a much bigger role than organisations in shaping our day-to-day experience.

Why do teams have three times the impact?

There are two main reasons that teams affect our happiness more than organisations:

1. Positivity resonance
2. The way we do things

1. Positivity resonance

The term *positivity resonance*, best attributed to Barbara Fredrickson (Fredrickson, 2013), refers to the way we catch the mood of the people around us. This can of course work both ways. We all know how annoying it is to work with an unhappy, selfish colleague who brings down everyone on the team. In contrast, it is a pleasure to work with a positive, collaborative colleague who lifts your spirits and helps you raise your game.

Some people call this the radiator-or-drain effect: positive people radiate their warmth and negative people drain our energy. Researchers have found that team leaders' moods are especially influential in this respect (Volmer, 2012). If you are a leader, be aware of your mood, as it will be resonating around your team.

2. The way we do things

Team culture itself – *the way they do things* – differs a lot, and those differences most certainly impact both team happiness and performance.

This is where the Five Ways are so helpful, emphasising to teams and team leaders the sort of things needed to make the team both happy and successful. Here's a reminder of the Five Ways:

1. **Connect** – build good relationships
2. **Be fair** – appreciate each other
3. **Empower** – share responsibility
4. **Challenge** – give helpful feedback
5. **Inspire** – accomplish meaningful goals together

All of these positive behaviours are very actionable at the team level. They don't need organisational directives and policies. Teams can make these Five Ways a part of the way they do things and become both happier and more successful.

There's one important caveat to the power of teams: size matters. My data shows that smaller teams – typically those with ten or fewer members – tend to have a stronger, more positive impact on people's happiness at work. There may not be a perfect team size, but in the next chapter, I'll explore what history, literature and real-world practice can teach us, drawing on insights from Shakespeare, the Chinese army and a Dutch healthcare provider.

Summary

- **Teams shape our everyday experience of work.** The biggest influence on our happiness at work isn't the organisation – it's the team. My data shows that team culture explains nearly three times more of the variation in individual happiness than organisational culture does.

- **Positivity is contagious – and local.** From positivity resonance to the 'radiator or drain' effect, our teammates' moods, and especially those of our team leaders, have a powerful impact on how we feel and perform.

- **Happiness bubbles up rather than trickles down.** Team-level behaviours, like the Five Ways, don't need top-down directives to flourish. When teams focus on connection, fairness, empowerment, challenge and inspiration, happiness bubbles up.

24
Size Matters, And Shakespeare Knew It

Shakespeare was a brilliant playwright. One of the key reasons his plays still resonate is that he was extraordinarily psychologically astute. As well as creating deep, complex characters and narratives, he also seemed to have an awareness that the audience could only deal with a certain amount of complexity. He regularly injected comic characters into his plays to help the audience take a break from the intensity. He also knew that to follow a dialogue, people could cope with only a limited number of characters interacting at the same time.

Today psychologists call this understanding *mentalising*, *theory of mind* or even sometimes *mindreading*. It is our capacity to see things from another person's perspective or 'hold them in mind'. Shakespeare seemed acutely aware of the limits of this human capacity. He typically kept conversations on stage to four characters or fewer and often reduced it to three when those characters were discussing someone else who wasn't present. Of course, there are exceptions – *A Midsummer Night's Dream* being a wonderfully chaotic case in point – but the general pattern is clear. I came across this insight in a fascinating paper, 'The small world of Shakespeare's plays' (Dunbar, Nettle and Stiller, 2003), which inspired much of my thinking here.

This limited capacity of humans might seem obscure, but we all experience it on a regular basis. Imagine you are at a networking event, chatting in a group of four. Another couple of people hover around, and being friendly, you widen the circle to let them join in. It is almost guaranteed that a side conversation will start after a couple of minutes, effectively splitting the group into two smaller ones. This is the limit in our capacity to mentalise in action – we can only hold about four other people in mind at the same time.

Trust is a complex cognitive process

Mentalising is also the very basis of trust. Professor Robin Dunbar, an evolutionary psychologist and anthropologist, articulates the slightly elusive concept of trust as a third-order mentalising process. That is to say, it requires a series of three intentional verbs to describe it: 'I *understand* that when you say you

The organisation that grew huge by keeping small

One of the best examples of an organisation that has put this into practice successfully and rapidly scaled is the Dutch community healthcare provider, Buurtzorg, Dutch for 'community organisation' (Laloux, 2014). The organisation was founded in 2007 by former nurse Jos de Blok, who was disenchanted with the nursing industry. He felt the industry had become like a manufacturing assembly line, with nurses assigned specific jobs and given strict quotas for how many minutes they could spend with each patient. Instead of a top-down approach, de Blok championed small teams of self-organising nurses, with a strict rule: any team that grew to ten people had to split into two groups.

The result? Buurtzorg grew from zero to a turnover of $275 million within eight years. It now has over 14,000 employees and is the largest healthcare provider in the Netherlands, three times the size of its nearest competitor. It's also been named the nation's best employer five times, based on regular employee surveys.

Understanding that size matters when it comes to teams sounds obvious, but it goes against the business idea of economies of scale. The optimal size of any team depends on a range of factors, including industry, culture and workload. However, it is important that teams are kept to a manageable size – a lesson that Google had to learn the hard way, which I will cover in the next chapter. As Buurtzorg successfully showed, if teams get much larger than ten, it is probably best to break them up into smaller units.

Summary

- **Smaller groups build stronger trust.** Our brains can only hold a handful of people in mind at once, which limits the size of conversations and makes trust easier to build in small teams.

- **Five is a functional group size.** From Shakespeare's stage to military units, history shows that small groups – around five people – allow for connection, creativity and cohesion.

- **Big growth can come from small teams.** Buurtzorg scaled to 14,000 employees by capping team size at ten, proving that keeping teams small can drive both culture and performance.

25
What Google Got Wrong About Team Leaders

Teams matter, as do people who lead teams, regardless of whether they are called team leaders, managers or supervisors. People in these roles are often undervalued in organisations and mocked in popular culture (think of the TV series *The Office* or the Dilbert cartoons).

Team leaders are uniquely positioned – close to their teams but also with a connection to the company's strategy – which makes them critical to both team happiness and business success. They are like your own internal influencers.

One organisation that undervalued them was Google, which might seem extraordinary due to their huge success, but this story comes at the start of their growth. In the early 2000s Google's senior leaders believed managers got in the way of their engineers and decided to scrap virtually all middle managers. At the time there were only about 300 engineers, and somewhat incredibly, Google decided that all those engineers would report to just one manager. This effectively created a single team of 300 people, though this was more likely a group of 300 independent individuals. Unsurprisingly, it was a policy that lasted only a couple of months. However, even as Google rapidly grew to tens of thousands of employees, there was still a mistrust, or at least a lack of respect, for managers. Rather brilliantly, and being true to their own data-led approach, Google decided to set up an internal research project to explore whether managers did matter.

During this period Google's people function was led by Laszlo Bock, who in 2015 published a best-selling book, *Work Rules!* (Bock, 2015). In it he explained how this research, which came to be called Project Oxygen, started out: 'Project Oxygen initially set out to prove that managers don't matter and ended up demonstrating that good managers were crucial.'[27]

The project name came from one of the researchers observing that 'having a good manager is essential, like breathing. And if we make managers better, it would be like a breath of fresh air.'

---

27 This quote and all subsequent ones are from Chapter 8 of the book.

Google's research is also like a breath of fresh air for me as a statistician, as it's all empirically based. Lots of leadership books are full of great ideas and advice, but the strength of the Project Oxygen research is that it had access to Google's internal figures on team performance, together with data on team members' experience. The researchers could even track the impact that people changing teams, and therefore managers, had on their performance. This sort of longitudinal within-person data is powerful, and it has similarities to the BT call operator research, referenced in Chapter 13, that was able to prove the causal link between happiness and sales.

The eight key attributes of a great manager

The Google research team first identified the best and worst managers. Using a series of questionnaires and interviews, the researchers then started to explore the qualities of the best managers. This gave them a list of the eight key attributes of great managers (Bock, 2015). All those marked with an asterisk are people skills:

1. Be a good coach*

2. Empower team and do not micromanage*

3. Express interest/concern for team members' success and personal wellbeing*

4. Be productive/results-oriented

5. Be a good communicator – listen and share information*

6. Help the team with career development*

7. Have a clear vision/strategy for the team

8. Have important technical skills that help advise the team

What I love about this list is that the Google team didn't have a preconceived model they were looking to verify; their findings just emerged out of the data. In many ways it is an entirely uncontroversial list – all of these qualities are perfectly reasonable things to expect from a team leader. However, it is in rank order of importance, and it is interesting that five of the top six are people skills.

People skills aren't soft; they are essential

People skills are often, somewhat dismissively, called 'soft', as if they are less important than 'hard' technical skills. However, Google – one of the foremost tech businesses ever, with thousands of engineers – found that 'of the behaviours that differentiated the very best, technical input made the smallest difference to teams' (Bock, 2015).

Think back to the ancient friend-or-foe assessment that I wrote about in Chapter 6. In making rapid social assessments, we first assess the warmth of the other person, shortly followed by judging their competence. Whilst team leadership is about building longer-term relationships, everyday interactions still matter, and having a team leader who has your best interests at heart makes a huge difference.

For Google the Oxygen project wasn't just a piece of research; it was data for them to action and improve their performance. In *Work Rules!* (Bock, 2015) Laszlo Bock explains that Google realised they needed to be more specific in their research. For example, while it seems obvious that the best managers are good coaches – number one on the list above – they also need to hold regular one-to-one meetings. At those one-to-ones, instead of just asking the team member how things were for them, the manager would ideally work with the employee to diagnose problems and find ideas tailored to their strengths.

They measured then they acted on the results

To support managers in improving their people skills, Google offered them courses such as Manager as Coach and Career Conversations to help them have different kinds of conversations with their team members. Over time there has been a steady improvement in their manager rating scores, including improving their approval rating from 83% to 88% within two years. For the bottom quartile there was an even larger improvement, from 70% to 77%. Google also followed up specific impacts of each specific course; for example, Manager as Coach improved coaching average scores by an average of 13%, and Career Conversations improved career development ratings by 10% (Bock, 2015).

It's easy for us to just gloss straight over these figures and not register how remarkable they are. 88% of people working at Google think their managers are doing a good job. While I don't use precisely the same question in my population surveys, I get very different levels of endorsement. For example, in the UK and USA only 66% of people rated their manager as doing well, with that rating for those in the bottom quartile of performance dropping to 25%.[28] Meanwhile, more than three-quarters of Google employees in the lowest performing teams still rated their manager well.

For Google to have their manager ratings scores so high across the board shows that they have been doing something right. That they value team leaders and managers was surely part of the reason they have become so successful. They understood that good managers were crucial to their success, and they invested in training managers to improve their essential people skills.

---

28 For the USA it is 67% and the UK 65%. These precise figures come from the 2017 global survey of 22,000 people that I carried out in conjunction with the global recruitment agency Robert Half. The cross-tabulation with performance data comes from the 2023 UK survey.

This is what is so refreshing about Google's measurement-led approach. They started out thinking that managers didn't matter, but when the data insights showed the opposite, they changed direction. They followed up their new insights with actions, and then in turn measured the impact of these changes. In Part Six I will introduce my own measurement-led process, which very much aligns with Google's approach.

Summary

- **The role of team leader is underestimated.** Google initially overlooked the importance of team leaders but later recognised that they are essential – not just for steering teams, but also for connecting people to the company's wider strategy and culture.

- **Google learned through listening.** By surveying employees, Google discovered that people skills – not technical expertise – were the key to effective leadership and to driving both happiness and performance.

- **Google turned insight into impact.** With targeted support and training, Google helped its managers develop their people skills, leading to consistently high ratings and a powerful lesson in valuing team leaders.

26
Leading A Team Isn't Easy

Building a happy, successful team is as much an art as it is a science. In this short chapter I want to acknowledge some of the main challenges faced by managers, especially those aiming to support their people while achieving their goals. It's not easy being a people leader. In fact, it's one of the hardest jobs in any organisation.

Being pulled in two directions

I'm going to start by asking you to picture a charioteer battling to control two headstrong horses. The image dates back to ancient Greece, where Plato used it to describe the inner conflict of the soul, but it's just as fitting for the daily reality of many team leaders: that familiar, exhausting sensation of being pulled in two directions at once.

This metaphor is especially relevant when it comes to building happy and successful teams. Think of the charioteer as the team leader, trying to steer the chariot – the team or business – forward. One horse pulls hard towards business goals, demanding focus, targets and performance. The other represents the wellbeing and happiness of the team, urging us towards connection, care and a sense of balance. Holding the reins of both, while keeping the wheels on, is a tough and often underappreciated balancing act.

I once heard a CEO of a scaling business describe this tension perfectly, saying that he feels he has two leadership personas. The first is a hippy, peace-and-love character, who wants his teams to be happy and fulfilled. The second is the persona of a seventeenth-century mill owner, wanting to squeeze every last drop of work out of his employees. He describes being pulled in two different directions at once and being aware that he was hopping between two personas.

That's why the image of a charioteer battling to control two headstrong horses is so powerful. It doesn't just illustrate the tension, it also contains the solution. The real skill lies in harnessing the energy of both horses – ambition and wellbeing – so that they pull in the same direction. When that happens, the chariot doesn't just move; it flies.

Summary

- **Leading a team is challenging and comes with multiple pressures.** You may sometimes feel yourself pulled in two different directions.

- **Every leader has their own 'two horses' to manage.** What do they look like for you, and which one is dominant?

- **The art of strong leadership lies in aligning performance and wellbeing.** What would it take to get both horses pulling in the same direction?

27
Time: The Currency Of Relationships

Time is a genuinely limited resource. All of us have tough choices about how we spend our time and what we focus on, but these dilemmas are especially acute for people leaders. A recent survey showed that for 48% of middle managers the top obstacle that prevented them from being better people managers was a lack of time (Schaninger, Hancock and Field, 2023). For team leaders to do a good job managing their teams, how they allocate their resources, including their precious time, is critical.

One way to think about time use is to go back to that image of a charioteer battling to control two horses. We can think of one horse as the performance of the team and the other as the team's happiness. The chariot will go forward fastest if they are aligned, but that can often feel difficult, not least because of time use and two very different ways of thinking about it.

The business mantra: Time is money

One of the most enduring business mantras over the last century has been *Time is money*. How teams and team leaders spend their time is critical to their performance. We need to be careful of language here, though, because when time is framed as money, it's easy to see it purely as a cost. Also, when something is seen as a cost, the natural instinct is to minimise it. There is a twist, though, as in the business world, it is *paid time* that counts as a cost; and since productivity is measured as value added per paid hour, work hours are often extended till the work is done.

This is how long-hours cultures can take a grip, especially in organisations that don't pay overtime.[29] The data backs this up, as in the UK managers work on average 6.4 hours of unpaid overtime a week, rising to over 11.4 hours for senior leaders (Office for National Statistics, 2024). Although many employees wish there were more hours in the day, there is little incentive for employers to change the pattern, as they are getting 15–20% more hours at no extra cost. Even the

---

29 Even paying overtime at the same hourly rate can result in this, as it is cheaper to get an extra ten hours a week out of four people than recruit, onboard and train a new person. This is partly why unions negotiate overtime to be paid at time and a half, ie 150% the normal rate.

UK's Trades Union Congress (TUC) – a federation of trade unions – commented in a recent report that 'the additional responsibilities of senior staff are not properly managed by employers' (TUC, 2023).

A new mantra: Time is the currency of relationships

The phrase *Time is money* has become so embedded in our business culture that it's hard to think of time spent at work as anything but a cost to the business. Some years ago, though, I was in a meeting about government policies on loneliness, when someone used a beautiful turn of phrase: *Time is the currency of relationships*.[30] It rather brilliantly subverts the idea of time being money into the non-financial realm of relationships. I think we all instantly recognise there is a truth in it. Friendships are built by spending time together. When we meet someone new, it takes an investment of time, from both sides, to become friends. Raising children also requires a lot of our time.

The problem is that time is a limited resource. Robin Dunbar, the primatologist and evolutionary psychologist, writes about seeing this effect in his research in his book *Friends* (Dunbar, 2021):

---

30 I heard this from John Ashcroft of The Relationships Foundation. In an email exchange while I was writing this book, he said 'I can't claim that it's necessarily original to us, though it's a phrase we've used frequently over the years. You can reference my use of it here, though: *The Relational Lens*' (Ashcroft et al, 2016).

'Time is a limited commodity, and the time we have available for social interaction is very much a zero-sum affair – the time we give to one friend is time that cannot be given to another. We know from our studies of both monkeys and humans that the quality of a friendship depends directly on the time we invest in it.'

The quality of team relationships is shaped in the same way, ie by the time we invest in them. This creates a real conundrum in the time-pressured world of work. It's hard to make time now, simply to build trust and connection, especially when results are expected immediately. If we want the two horses of performance and wellbeing to pull in the same direction, though, we need to reframe how we see time. Time spent with your team isn't a cost to minimise – it's an investment in the social capital that drives future success. Neglecting that investment is like running down your capital reserves to fund short-term operations. It might keep you afloat temporarily, but it's not sustainable.

Three Greek gods of time

In the previous chapter, I introduced the ancient Greek image of the chariot – a powerful metaphor for the tension team leaders feel as they try to steer between competing demands. It's fitting to stay with the Greeks a moment longer, as they had an equally rich and layered understanding of time. For them time wasn't just something to track with a clock – it came in different forms, each with its own meaning and power. In fact, they had three distinct gods of time – Chronos, Aion and Kairos – each offering a unique lens on how we lead, connect and use our time wisely:

- **Chronos** is the best known of these three gods. He is normally depicted as an old man with an hourglass, and we might these days call him Father Time. We get the word *chronological* from this god, and he represents the empirical linear time that passes.

- **Aion** was the god of eternal time – the time of the heavens that is both infinite and cyclical. He is normally drawn as a youth with a serpent coiled around his arm. We get the word *aeons* from him, and he represents the repeating pattern of days, months, years and ages.[31]

- **Kairos** was the god of opportune moments, or 'the right time'. Unlike Chronos and Aion, Kairos represents the idea of a critical, decisive moment rather than the continuous passing of time. He was depicted as a young man, often with wings on his feet and a tuft of hair on his forehead,

---

31 I must admit to being disappointed that Aion isn't a goddess. For a brilliant exploration of cyclical time that includes feminine and indigenous perspectives, I highly recommend the book *Pip Pip* (Griffiths, 1999).

which could be seized by a person when it came within reach but could not be grasped again.[32]

Time, rhythm and opportunity

These three kinds of time offer complementary perspectives on how we build strong relationships within teams and workplaces:

- **Chronos** reminds us that investing consistent time with colleagues is essential.
- **Aion** suggests that these interactions should follow a predictable rhythm, creating a sense of flow and continuity.
- **Kairos** highlights the importance of seizing key moments, ensuring that when opportunities for connection arise, we make the most of them.

Taken together, they show that good working relationships don't just happen – they are nurtured over time, through both regularity and responsiveness. The trick is to find a balance between structure and spontaneity, investing the time and making the most of it.

---

32 Kairos reminds me of the character played by Robin Williams, John Keating, in the film *Dead Poets Society*, who passionately tells his pupils to 'seize the day', using the Latin phrase 'carpe diem'. The Romans didn't have a specific god/goddess that captured this, though Occasio was a symbolic figure in Roman art and literature. She, like Kairos, represents the fleeting nature of opportunities and was often also depicted with a forelock.

Summary

- **Time is a limited resource, especially for people leaders.** It's not just about having too much to do. The real challenge is how to prioritise what matters. If time is always seen as a cost, relationships will suffer. If we reframe time as the currency of relationships, then investing time in your team becomes the smartest, most strategic use of it.

- **Good relationships need consistency, rhythm and presence.** Drawing on the Greek gods of time – Chronos (consistency), Aion (rhythm) and Kairos (presence) – we can see that great team cultures are built over time, with regular moments of connection and a readiness to seize key opportunities.

- **Reimagining time use is essential.** Time spent with your team isn't a nice-to-have or a reward after the 'real work' – it is the work. Relationships are what make teams function. Reclaiming time for people isn't indulgent; it's wise. That's how the chariot really moves forward.

28
The Seven Successes Of Happy Teams

In the nautical world it is common to talk about captains running a happy ship. That is a high compliment to the ship's commander, indicating not only that his crew have high morale, but also that they are functioning well together, ensuring both safety and success. I am sure the captain's job is then also much happier – a mutinous crew is of course perilous.

Running a happy team is the same. It should be seen a high compliment to run a happy team that is functioning well and successful. They are also a lot less stressful to lead than an unhappy team, even if it's highly unlikely they will rise up and throw their leader overboard. Much more likely is that they will jump ship and join another company.

As evidenced in Chapter 25, people in great teams feel much better managed than those in teams that are less happy or successful. They also are much more likely to say they get along well with their team leader. Leading a happy ship is the way to be a happy captain!

The Seven Successes

In earlier chapters I've shared lots of ways that happiness improves business outcomes. When I gather these all together, I call them the *Seven Successes of Happy Teams*:

1. **Stability.** Happy teams are more stable. They have lower levels of staff turnover, which creates continuity of team members. This not only lowers recruitment costs; it also helps create more stable relationships with other teams, customers and suppliers.

2. **Energy.** Happy teams are energetic teams. They have a positive energy about them and get things done. In contrast, OK teams are low-energy, and burning-out ones are running on empty.

3. **Collaboration.** Happy teams collaborate better, both within the team and with other teams. They communicate better, support each other and work in connection with each other.

4. **Creativity.** Happy teams are more creative. They respect each other's opinions and ideas, enabling

them to build ideas and find more innovative solutions to the challenges they face.

5. **Attraction.** Happy teams attract good things towards them. This includes talented applicants for roles, support from other teams when needed, and even the attraction of prospective customers. Note: Attraction isn't referring here to looks, although a smile is surely much more attractive than a scowl.

6. **Effectiveness.** Happy teams are more effective. They consistently achieve their goals and are more productive. Both the quantity and quality of their work are better.

7. **Profit.** Happy teams create a surplus, as they generate more value at lower cost than OK or unhappy teams. Ultimately, they contribute more to profits and to stakeholder value.

The Seven Successes are the benefits you can unlock by promoting team happiness. They sure make running a team much more enjoyable too.

Summary

- **A happy ship works best.** Like a well-run crew at sea, happy teams work better together. They also make leadership a lot more enjoyable (and far less stressful).

- **Happiness drives success in seven ways.** From stability to creativity and from energy to profit, happy teams consistently outperform in seven essential areas.

- **Success provides an all-round better team.** The Seven Successes don't just boost results; they also make leading a team more rewarding, less stressful and a whole lot more fun.

PART FIVE
THE BAD AND THE UGLY

29
Three Personal Factors We Often Overlook

Up until now I have focused mainly on the 'good' outcomes that come from team happiness. In this part I will switch attention to 'the bad and the ugly' – the things that can and do go wrong, either by employee happiness being ignored or due to misguided interventions. Happiness can seem elusive, and our ability to predict what will impact our future happiness is especially suspect. This is why I like empirical studies so much, as they can provide us with evidence that help us make better decisions.

While most of this book is about how happiness at work is a collective endeavour, there is also a personal side we can't ignore. In this chapter I'll explore three factors that focus on us as individuals:

1. Working isn't bad for us
2. Which team you join really matters
3. Long commutes drain us more than we think

1. Working isn't bad for us

Work is often seen as a necessary evil or at least an unavoidable burden. It's something many of us feel we have to endure in order to earn the money we need to live the rest of our lives. Our use of the language highlights this mindset – in English the adjective most often paired with the word *work* is 'hard'!

Where would we be without work, though? Being unemployed is miserable. In fact, it is three times worse than can be explained by loss of income alone, as illustrated in the article 'Unhappiness and Unemployment' (Clark and Oswald, 1994). Work doesn't only pay the bills; it also helps us feel useful, brings us into the realm of relationships and provides a structure to our lives. This is probably why some people become a bit lost when they retire, losing a sense of purpose and missing the social environment. It's also why volunteering can enrich our lives, even if it doesn't increase our income.

However, just because no work is bad, it doesn't mean that all jobs are good for us. There are, quite frankly, some sh*t jobs out there. There are also a lot of great ones, though. It's obviously better to have a good job that you enjoy, but that raises the question: How much better is a good job? One recent study has explored precisely this question, using data from the European Working Conditions Survey (EWCS), which is based on interviews with more than 40,000 people across Europe (Eurofound, 2019). By comparing effect sizes, Professor Francis Green from University College London has shown that job quality is just as important as our health for our overall wellbeing in life (Green et al, 2024). The graph below shows the comparative impacts.

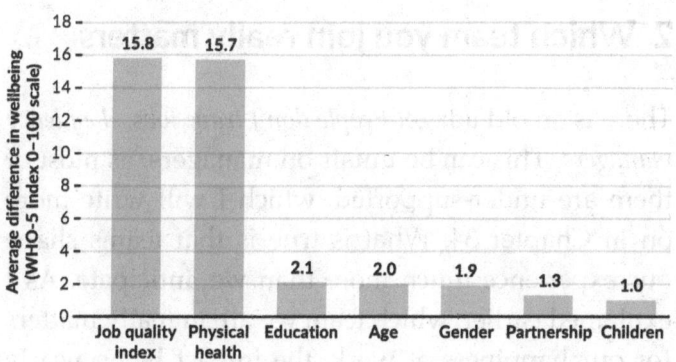

Effect of job quality and other life domains on wellbeing, WHO-5 Index 0–100 scale
(Source: 'Work and Life' (Green et al, 2024))

Having a good job is just as important as good health for our overall happiness and wellbeing. Green also compares the effect size to demographic factors like age, gender and relationship status. However, the partnership variable captures only whether someone is in a relationship, not its quality. In contrast, the work and health questions do ask about quality, which helps explain their stronger impact. If the survey had included relationship quality, its influence on happiness would likely have been just as strong – if not stronger – than job or health quality.

The take-home message is that if you want to live a good life, finding a good job is as important as having good health, and a job is about much more than only your income level.

2. Which team you join really matters

There is an old adage: *People don't leave jobs; they leave managers.* This can be unfair on managers, as most of them are under-supported, which I will write more on in Chapter 34. What is true is that teams shape our experience much more than we anticipate. As I explained earlier, which team we are in really matters for our happiness at work, the impact being nearly three times bigger than that of the organisation.

It is good to remember this whenever you are changing roles. Think about the team you will be joining. Ask in interviews how happy the team is that you would be joining. Maybe ask to spend a day with them before accepting the role. Watch out for red flags such as poor communication, little enthusiasm, or people just seeming exhausted. Ask people what they love about their work, and (if you dare) what they don't. All of this is important information.

Happiness is all about good fit, so give yourself the best chance of being happy and successful in your new role by choosing your future team well.

3. Long commutes drain us more than we think

Daniel Kahneman, the renowned psychologist, created a new way of measuring people's wellbeing in 2004 (Kahneman et al, 2004). Called Day Reconstruction Methodology, it asked people to write down every activity they did on a particular day and also rate how much they enjoyed every activity. Consistently, the least happy activity was the commute to work, and the second least happy was the commute back home. Kahneman's original work didn't look at the impact of different lengths of commutes, but others have, and there seems to be a threshold when the impact gets much worse. That threshold is a journey time of around one hour or fifty miles, depending on how it was measured (Chatterjee, 2020).

There are a couple of caveats to this. If a significant portion of the commute is active, for example walking or cycling, the impact is much less. The second is that long commutes – over about three hours – don't have a negative impact, probably because people use the commuting time productively.

We all only have 168 hours in a week, and if we spend a significant portion of that time on an unhappy, unproductive commute, it will drain us over time. It is also undoubtedly a major reason people like working from home. However, as I will discuss later, working from home isn't necessarily better for our happiness at work or in life. There is evidence that people's mental health can deteriorate if they work fully remotely (Gueguen and Senik, 2023). Working in the same room as colleagues is a richer experience, just like watching a band live is very different from watching them on video.

Summary

- **Good jobs are as important as good health.** Work gives us more than just income – it supports our wellbeing, identity and structure in life. When job quality is high, its impact on happiness rivals even our health.

- **The team you join shapes your experience.** Teams influence our happiness at work three times more than the wider organisation. When changing jobs, choosing the right team is crucial.

- **Long commutes quietly erode wellbeing.** Commutes of over an hour, especially if passive, can significantly reduce happiness. It's a drain many underestimate – one reason remote and hybrid working appeals to so many.

30
The Cost Of Ignoring Team Happiness

How employees feel about their work, especially when they don't care and don't take care, will expose organisations of all shapes and sizes to risks they would rather avoid. Senior leaders may use different terms such as *mitigating risks* or *building resilience*, but they won't be very effective if team happiness is overlooked.

Different sectors face different risks. Educators will worry about poor student grades, manufacturers about product quality and banks about fraud. However, there are three major risks common to all sectors, and a focus on team happiness will help avoid the disruption they can cause.

Three main risks: Underperformance, flight and burnout

Senior leaders tend to worry most about two critical risks: underperformance and high levels of employee turnover. Employees, especially team leaders, will also feel the risk of burnout acutely, which will lead to lower performance and employees leaving or going on long-term sick leave. In this chapter I am going to look at how changes in team happiness predict these risks, and that they can act as an early warning system for organisations.

The BT call operator study mentioned in Chapter 13 showed definitively that changes in happiness led to changes in performance. On sunnier weeks operators were happier, and they sold more than in weeks when the weather was gloomy. The weather made only a small impact on their moods, but the large numbers surveyed were sufficient to find proof of the causal pathway. In the study it was estimated that the weather changes could explain about 6% of the variance in people's moods. Think of the impact that could be made by intentional changes to improve teams' happiness, rather than leaving it to random changes in the weather.

In Chapter 12 I also shared data that tracked employee happiness within one large 9,000-person business. It showed that employees who were unhappy in one quarter were more than three times more likely to leave the very next quarter than their happier colleagues. That clearly shows the predictive value of this type of data, especially as teams shape people's experience, so flight risk will vary between teams.

Feeling emotionally exhausted from work is far too common an experience; however it is difficult, even for the person experiencing it, to recognise when burnout is starting to take hold. The red flags are often present, but they can be overridden, especially when people feel committed to their work. The data I shared in Chapter 18 on happiness and burnout was from a cross-sectional survey of the UK working population so showed only an association between the two factors. To move beyond association and towards early detection, I've recently completed a new analysis of our client data, with the aim of identifying the key predictors of burnout before it takes hold.

Using happiness data to predict these key risks

In early 2024 I asked our clients' permission to add some questions to their regular surveys for my research purposes. In that module I included some questions on their recent experience of burnout as well the same question about team performance that I introduced in Chapter 21. For staff turnover I didn't need to ask whether people were thinking of leaving as I could track actual departures over time.

The data I gathered was further confirmation of how important happiness is for key business outcomes. However, for my analysis I didn't have to rely on just the team happiness scores; I could also use data from the fifteen questions in teams' culture profiles (based on the Five Ways). I used a technique called *pathway analysis*, more formally known as *structural equation modelling*, to estimate how much of the variance in outcomes is directly attributable to given variables; and how much is indirectly attributable, mediated by happiness. I identified the five variables that, together with team happiness, best predicted underperformance, flight and burnout. The table below shows them and their impact on each of these three critical risks.

Risk factors for underperformance, staff turnover and burnout

	Underperformance	Flight	Burnout
Happiness	X	XX	
Team cooperation	X		
Work-life balance		O	XX
Appreciation		X	X
Helpful feedback	X		
Sense of accomplishment	X		

Note: XX: major risk (twice the strength); X: risk factor; O: some risk (half strength)

The risk of underperformance is driven by low happiness, poor cooperation between teams, a lack of helpful feedback and low accomplishment.

Flight risk is mainly driven by general unhappiness, but a lack of appreciation is a contributing factor, and low work–life balance also adds a small amount of additional risk.

Burnout is not directly related to unhappiness, probably because people who enjoy their work are more prone to overdoing it. Instead, burnout is directly related to poor work–life balance and a lack of appreciation.

The great thing about this analysis is that I have been able to create algorithms for our clients to identify which of their teams are at risk. I can literally add (virtual) red flags to the results to grab their attention.

Ignoring team happiness increases a whole myriad of risks for organisations. Collecting data on team happiness can act as an early warning system so leaders can help mitigate risks before they become too disruptive. It's further evidence that happiness isn't just a nice-to-have; it's essential for business success.

In the next chapter I will turn to some of the most common ways of trying to promote a 'fun' culture at work: ping-pong, pizza and parties.

Summary

- **Businesses face three core risks.** Underperformance, staff turnover and burnout are big risks facing any organisation, and all three are closely linked to team happiness.

- **Happiness predicts outcomes.** Team happiness is a strong early indicator of flight risk and underperformance. Burnout is more closely tied to poor work–life balance and low appreciation.

- **Data aids prevention.** Tracking team happiness and culture provides an early warning system, allowing organisations to address risks before they escalate.

31
The Three Ps: Ping-pong, Pizza And Parties

I'm not trying to be the Grinch here – I love a good party as much as the next guy. I'm also partial to a bit of pizza and have been known to get overly competitive at ping-pong. Let's be honest, though: these extras – the three Ps – aren't going to build happy teams on their own.

I was talking to a group of CEOs once, and one of them immediately equated happiness interventions with ping-pong tables. He said something along the lines of, 'I bought my team a ping-pong table. When I walk past it and no one is playing, I think *What a waste of money*. Then when I walk past and people are playing, I think *Why are they not working?*'

He most definitely saw this as a lose-lose situation rather than the win-win that's at the heart of building happy teams. As well as ping-pong tables not being particularly effective, they also risk employees being treated like overgrown kids, providing distraction rather than addressing what really drives team happiness.

In a way, this reflects how the power relationship between employers and employees has changed over the century. In the 1920s work was scarce and people needed to work to escape poverty, so employers didn't really need to address workers' needs except in their salaries. The relationship was reminiscent of that of a master and servant. By the mid-twentieth century, especially due to pressure from unions, this dynamic had started to change, and improvements were made in working conditions, pensions and insurance policies. Personnel departments were created to look after employees, though this was mainly in a sort of paternalistic way, where the employer was effectively the parent and the employee the child.

Don't treat employees like children (or teenagers)

In her book *HR Disrupted* (Adams, 2017), the ex-HR director of the BBC, Lucy Adams, writes well about this and why the employer-as-parent model needs a shakeup:

'This wouldn't be so bad if we in HR carried out our parental duties consistently, but if we're trying to behave like parents we're doing a pretty bad job of it. Financial pressure means we're making people redundant, cutting their pay and pensions, and reducing their benefits. Families don't do that to each other, do they?'

She goes on to explain that the problem is deeper – the employer-as-parent model is no longer sustainable, and it creates a situation where employees feel unable to challenge authority, speak up or take risks.

Many progressive leaders instinctively recognise that the parent–child relationship is unsustainable, but instead of moving to an adult–adult relationship, many organisations seem to get stuck in between, thinking that they need a parent–teenager-type relationship. Facebook seemed to take this idea to its logical conclusion by offering a laundry service for its employees, I guess with the logic that it would free up more time for them to work, though I imagine they talked in terms of removing friction from people's lives. That's very infantilising, though. Unsurprisingly, in the recent difficult economic climate Facebook announced they were discontinuing the free laundry service, along with several other perks such as free dinners (Yang, 2022).

As I said, I'm no Grinch, and pizzas and parties certainly have their place. If your team is working on a project that requires a period of overtime, of course it's appropriate to order in food and to have a party to celebrate its completion. If there is a permanent long-hours culture, though, no amount of pizza is going to mitigate the risk of teams burning out. Parties are similar in that they can boost happiness scores, but the effect is very short-term.

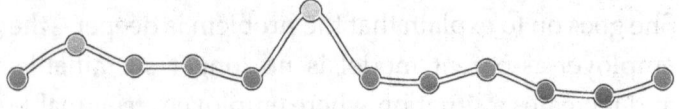

Impact of a party on organisational happiness

Above is a graph showing the happiness time trend of one of our clients. They had an all-company party one week, in October rather than in the most common time, the run-up to Christmas. This helps because it's hard to see a pure effect of parties held around year end due to so much else going on at that time. You can see from the peak in the graph that everyone loved the party. Their happiness score rose to 90, which means the vast majority of the 100+ employees said they were 'very happy' at work last week. The party certainly boosted happiness levels, but only for one week. You can see that their scores returned back to their more normal (if still very good) levels the very next week. This organisation is consistently in the healthy upper zone, which indicates they have a great culture that supports happy and successful teams. An annual party is undoubtedly a part of their culture, but having an occasional party is not what keeps them in the healthy upper zone – that will be due to the way they work together every week.

Summary

- **Fun extras don't fix culture.** Ping-pong, pizza and parties can be enjoyable, but they don't address the deeper drivers of team happiness and performance. Distraction isn't the same as motivation.

- **Employees shouldn't be treated like kids.** Perks that feel patronising – like laundry services or constant freebies – can infantilise teams. Today's employees want to be treated as capable adults, not dependants.

- **It's important to focus on long-term foundations, not short-term boosts.** A well-timed party can lift spirits briefly, but only strong team culture sustains happiness week after week. The real work is in how people work together.

32
Most Wellbeing Programmes Don't Work

While organisations may underestimate the risks of employee unhappiness, many of them do at least introduce wellbeing programmes. However, although they are probably well intended, most of them have virtually no effect.

Analysing the impact of wellbeing programmes

I heard a story from the former European vice-president for Twitter, Bruce Daisley, when we were both speaking at a conference. In his talk he shared a photograph from a busy British hospital, which was promoting a free 'resilience workshop' for staff.[33] He explained that it evoked absolute rage from employees as they were under so much pressure. They felt that instead of fixing the system, management were trying to shift the responsibility back onto staff by saying that they should just learn to be more resilient. You can understand why they weren't happy.

This is an issue that goes far beyond the stresses of working in frontline healthcare. In a large analysis of wellbeing programmes, Dr William Fleming from Oxford University's Wellbeing Research Centre has shown that nearly all workplace wellbeing programmes have no positive impact, and courses in resilience actually had a negative impact (Fleming, 2024). That may sound like a harsh conclusion, but it's worth digging into the findings. While the results pose a challenge to many wellbeing providers, the analysis is robust and grounded in solid data.

Fleming's study was based on responses from 46,000 employees across 233 different UK workplaces. All the organisations were part of Britain's Healthiest Workplace survey, conducted by health and life insurance company Vitality between 2014 and 2024. As well as employees' responses, the survey gathered information from organisations on their internal wellbeing strategies. As these organisations all opted

---

[33] He has written a book about resilience, *Fortitude* (Daisley, 2022), though this particular story isn't from it.

in, we can be sure that they are among the most wellbeing-aware in the UK. If anybody was getting it right, surely it would be them? The organisations indeed offered a variety of wellbeing programmes, but once Fleming had crunched the numbers, there wasn't much good news.

The chart below shows the impact of those programmes on people's wellbeing. The beta values indicate the strength and direction of the effect, with larger values reflecting stronger associations.[34] Fleming also calculated the upper and lower 'credible' limits for these beta values (the Bayesian equivalent of 95% confidence intervals), which are shown as faint lines extending from each central marker – often called *whiskers* or *whispers*. These illustrate the range within which the true value is likely to fall. You'll notice that nearly all the whiskers cross the vertical (zero) axis. This means there is no statistical evidence that these interventions make any real impact on wellbeing, as the effect could be positive or negative. To emphasise this, I have highlighted the only two interventions that are statistically significant.

---

[34] Fleming used a multitude of measures in his study, the main one being the Warwick-Edinburgh Mental Wellbeing Scale. This is a superb, freely available measurement tool, which captures not only how people feel but also how they are functioning. It is widely used in the UK, and I used versions of it in my previous policy work. For more details see 'The Warwick-Edinburgh Mental Well-being Scale' (Tennant et al, 2007).

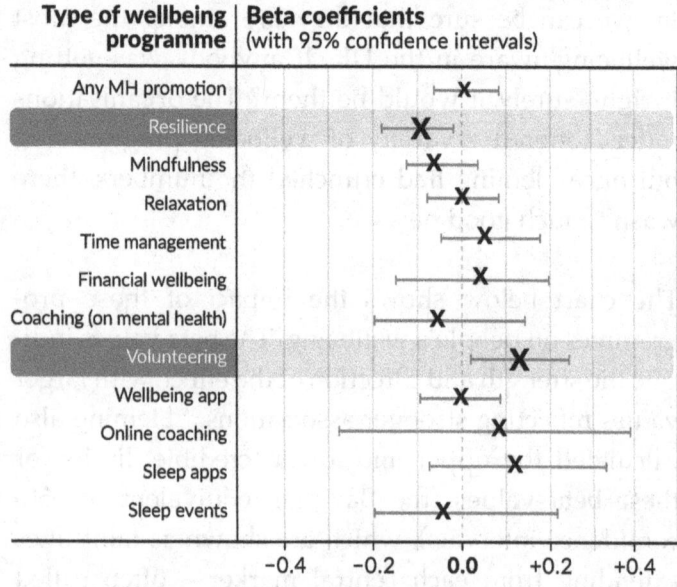

Impact of wellbeing programmes on individual wellbeing

The only programme that showed much promise was the one giving employees the opportunity to volunteer on social projects outside of work. The others had no significant impact, except resilience programmes, which were shown to *undermine* people's wellbeing.

This is quite astonishing, as resilience programmes are a billion-dollar industry, and they of course sound a sensible idea. The US military has been a particularly big spender in this area, with the recognition that military personnel need to be mentally as well as physically fit, especially as veterans have a shockingly high suicide rate. According to the '2022 National Veteran Suicide Prevention' report, veterans are nearly twice as likely to die by suicide than the rest of the US, with more than 6,000 dying in 2022 (VA, 2022).

To much fanfare, the US Army launched the Comprehensive Soldier Fitness programme, which cost more than $500 million to deliver. It was based on the work of Martin Seligman and the Penn Resilience Program, which itself started as a project to build resilience in school children (Penn Arts & Sciences, no date). It was always going to be quite a stretch to move from the classroom to the battlefield, and the programme simply didn't work for the US Army. There was no reduction in post-traumatic stress disorder or suicide levels. It didn't reduce the prescription of medications or addictions. It was a mandatory programme for a time, but as soon as it became voluntary, virtually no one signed up.[35]

I think the issue with these types of training and intervention is that they only sound like a great idea. They signal that the organisation cares, that they recognise there is an issue, and by putting their money where their mouths are, they're showing a genuine willingness to respond. However, these types of programmes have been oversold by providers, they often don't address the underlying causes, and their impact isn't assessed.

---

35 For an excellent critique of resilience training programmes, see Chapter Five of *Fortitude* (Daisley, 2022).

Dr Fleming's analysis suggests that the vast majority of spending on wellbeing programmes has little to no effect. His study also shows the power of measurement. I'm sure that most people who access these services are appreciative, and some might even write enthusiastic endorsements of them, but when proper measurement is introduced, the effect sizes are non-existent or minimal. This is why I think all businesses should measure the impact of any wellbeing programmes on their employees' happiness and wellbeing. You might then identify that this sort of intervention does work for you and your teams, and if you have the data that backs that up, then great. However, beware of offering overstretched staff resilience training, as it will almost certainly enrage them. In my opinion, their rage would be fully justified.

Summary

- **Most wellbeing programmes fall flat.** Despite good intentions, large-scale research shows that the majority of workplace wellbeing initiatives have no measurable impact on employee wellbeing. Some, like resilience training, can even make things worse.

- **Measurement matters.** Without robust evaluation, even the most well-meaning interventions can be misleading. Dr Fleming's study demonstrates how proper analysis can reveal the true (often disappointing) effects of popular programmes.

- **Meaningful change needs systemic action.** One-off interventions won't shift the dial if the root causes are left untouched. Overwork, lack of support and weak team culture are the real drivers of unhappiness, and fixing these requires systemic action.

33
Bad Systems Beat Good People

In Chapter 7, on the friction and flow in people's everyday work, I referred to a survey where I included a question asking what had frustrated people in the previous week. There were lots of complaints about relationships, whether with managers, colleagues or customers, plus naturally many people referring to overwork and long hours.

Frustrating IT systems

In addition to the frustrations around relationships and work levels, nearly a quarter of all complaints were about poor systems, including:

- **Tech issues** – especially slow, outdated or malfunctioning computers
- **System crashes** – internet freezes, network issues and downtime
- **Process inefficiencies** – unreliable, time-consuming systems and duplication of processes
- **Excessive admin** – paperwork, red tape and slow approval systems
- **Resource shortages** – missing materials and stock or supply chain issues

One particular response resonated: 'The systems are next-level bad – it's a battle to get anything done.' This reminded me of a quote from W Edward Denning: 'A bad system will beat a good person every time' (Hunter, 2015). Denning was a famous management guru, who in the 1950s helped rebuild the Japanese manufacturing sector, before returning to the US and championing ideas like total quality management.

Battling bad systems is a source of great frustration. Another respondent, a nurse, wrote, 'Paperwork, especially when having to take blood – the form is so time-consuming – super annoying.' This person was still using a paper-based system, but often electronic systems are no better. In one US study, researchers focused on the link between health professionals' mental health and their use of electronic health record

(EHR) systems. On a standardised scale for ease of use, the respondents ranked the system firmly in the 'not acceptable' range.[36] These highly paid and highly skilled physicians were spending more time doing admin than seeing patients and having to do extra unpaid overtime most days to just keep up. Unsurprisingly, there was a strong link to burnout, and the authors recommended that improving usability of systems should be considered to improve physicians' mental health (Melnick et al, 2020).

Improving IT and admin systems should be considered a happiness intervention. Quite clearly, when done well, they help teams be both happier and more successful.

A success story from an Irish county council

In mid-2024 I was giving a keynote at a conference in Ireland, and as is sometimes the case when I go to workplace wellbeing conferences, there was a series of local organisational case studies. There is a lot of good work going on out there, though sometimes I wonder if initiatives would pass the Fleming test

---

36 The scale is called a *system usability scale*, and this EHR system scored 45/100. For comparison, a Google search rated as 93, a microwave 87, an ATM machine 82, a GPS system 71 and an Excel spreadsheet 57. See 'The Association Between Perceived Electronic Health Record Usability and Professional Burnout Among US Physicians' (Melnick et al, 2020).

mentioned in Chapter 32, ie whether they actually improve people's mental health. Regardless, they are nearly always interesting.

There was one presentation at this particular conference that took me by surprise, especially as it was from an unlikely source: a local government authority; Clare County Council, to be precise. The speaker was one of the council's HR executives, and instead of talking about their wellbeing programme, she focused on how they had created better and easier systems for employees to use.

A lot of the Clare County Council staff work out in the community. Some are social workers visiting housing schemes. Others are doing emergency repairs on roads or other infrastructure. Those people used to have to complete paperwork or come back to the office to upload reports to the computer system, but then the council invested in a new tablet-based system to capture the data. This not only increased the quality of the information gathered; it also reduced by over 30% the amount of time that people spent doing admin.

This is a great example of a real win-win, and it's perhaps no surprise that the council won an excellence award, awarded by CIPD Ireland, for their working practices (Clare County Council, 2023). I can imagine that those health professionals in the US study – and anyone else – would be delighted to regain such a large portion of their time this way.

I often talk about the need to be systematic in building team happiness. This chapter is a reminder that the systems teams use are also vital.

Summary

- **Broken systems break morale.** Frustrating tech, inefficient processes and excessive admin are common workplace complaints. They are also major sources of unhappiness that drain energy and productivity.

- **Fixing systems is a happiness intervention.** Poor IT systems don't just slow people down – they contribute directly to stress and burnout. Improving usability can be a powerful way to support mental health and performance – one that is often overlooked.

- **Smart investments deliver major impact.** Clare County Council's success shows how thoughtful system upgrades can cut admin time by 30%, freeing up people's time and boosting both morale and efficiency.

34
A Disregard For Managers

In Chapter 25 I looked at how Google initially overlooked the importance of team leaders. They are not alone. In this chapter I'll dig into a wider issue: the surprisingly low level of attention many organisations give to their managers.

Accidental managers

Here's a troubling statistic. Despite the critical role they play, 80% of managers have absolutely no management training. This means the vast majority of leaders are, according to the UK's Chartered Management Institute (CMI), 'accidental managers'.

While I am always a little sceptical of these sorts of claims, I've checked this one out and have to say I agree. CMI back the claim with statistics from the UK's Employer Skills Survey, which has been conducted regularly since 2011. The survey shows that only 60% of employers provide any sort of training, and of those less than a third offer management (or supervisory) training (DfE, 2023). This means that only about 20% of managers have been trained, hence the CMI claim that 80% are accidental. It is quite shocking, really, especially as the amount offered is the lowest since they started gathering this data.

This phenomenon isn't just a UK issue. A US report (Cappelli, 2015) found that only 21% of employees had received any formal training in the last five years – perhaps an even worse scenario than in the UK.

In practice these reports reflect that the vast majority of team leaders are promoted and then just left to sink or swim. Some of course will be natural people leaders, but as Google found out, essential people skills can be improved with courses such as their Manager as Coach training. However, Google's hard-earned insights don't seem to have had much influence; most organisations continue to undervalue – or even neglect – their team leaders.

Middle management hollowed out

The number and importance of middle-level managers has been reduced over time (McIntosh, 2013). This hollowing-out is often presented as an efficiency exercise and has been championed by many large consultancy firms such as McKinsey's. It is more than a little ironic that three of their consultants recently published a book called *Power to the Middle* (Schaninger, Hancock and Field, 2023), in which they are highly critical of senior leaders for neglecting their managers:

> 'Too many executives are undercutting their managers, and they're losing money in the process because too many employees are not being developed to their full potential. We have come across large organisations – with tens of thousands of employees and billions in revenue – that have seemingly forgotten to take care of and develop their middle managers.'

The consultants go on to say it is no surprise that managers don't know how to manage, as they are effectively left to learn by osmosis. The situation was exacerbated during the Covid pandemic, when managers suddenly needed to support widely dispersed teams, often without any guidance on how to do that.

Managers as internal influencers

Expecting managers to learn without guidance is the sink-or-swim attitude in action, and it is neither effective nor fair. It's a miserly and miserable recipe for both underperformance and unhappiness. It is also particularly shortsighted, as managers have a multiplier effect – they are effectively internal influencers. Their people skills (or lack of) influence their whole team's experience of work. Indeed, they also – for better or worse – show potential future managers how to be people leaders.

Organisations that do leadership well value their team leaders. Google, for example, have adopted a systematic, measurement-led approach that supports team leaders to develop their people skills and to help their team members achieve their potential.

Not every organisation has the budget of a tech giant like Google, but there are other, lower-cost ways to learn, and measurement can support these. If you track team happiness and feed that data back to teams and team leaders, you can create a continuous learning process. Effectively, feedback is gathered, listened to and acted on. If done well, it can be a fun and rewarding process, as teams get to understand each other and work better together. As with everything about team happiness, it is a win-win situation.

Summary

- **Accidental managers aren't ideal leaders.** Around 80% of team leaders receive no formal management training, leaving most to learn by trial and error. This is often at the expense of their team's wellbeing and performance.

- **Middle management matters.** Years of cost cutting have hollowed out middle management layers, but research shows these roles are crucial for employee development, team culture and organisational success.

- **Managers can act as multipliers.** When supported and trained, managers become powerful internal influencers. Measuring and improving team happiness gives them the feedback they need to grow, benefiting the whole team.

35
Meaning Isn't Enough

In his famous speech of 1963, Martin Luther King first introduced the phrase: 'Even though we face the difficulties of today and tomorrow, I still have a dream.' His dream was about social justice and fairness, citing the US Declaration of Independence, 'We hold these truths to be self-evident, that all men are created equal.'

Today we clearly still have many difficulties of today and tomorrow, and the rise of purpose-led organisations is to be much welcomed. Meaning and purpose are great for motivating people, and they form the core of the *inspire* element of the Five Ways, but we shouldn't lose sight of the fact there can also be no happiness without fairness.[37] Too often, organisa-

---

37 This phrasing is inspired by Issac Prilleltensky, who coined the phrase 'there is no wellness without fairness' (Prilleltensky, 2012).

tions and sectors seem to exploit people's desire to do meaningful work, expecting them to accept lower pay or tougher conditions simply because the cause is noble. That's a bold statement but one that rings true for many of us who have chosen meaningful career paths over more financially rewarding ones. Is that fair? Probably the answer is: it depends.

The idea that work should be more than a curse can be traced back to the man Martin Luther King was named after: Martin Luther.[38] Luther suggested that if work pleased God and helped others, we should see it as a calling. It has been a profoundly influential idea and has become known as the *Protestant work ethic*. Today even agnostics and atheists can have a strong sense that work is an important way of contributing to society.

Psychologists call this people's *intrinsic motivation*, which is fuelled by our personal values and the inherent meaning of the activity we are engaged in. In contrast, *extrinsic motivation* is driven by external rewards such as money, recognition or the need to conform. Many people, from all walks of life, want to do work that they feel is meaningful, and my analyses show that these factors make a large contribution to people's happiness at work. However, seeing work as a calling can cause a problem, in that we sacrifice our

---

38 Martin Luther King was originally christened Michael Luther King. However, his father travelled to Germany in 1934 and was inspired by the original Martin Luther, and on his return changed his own and his five-year-old son's names to Martin Luther King.

own needs too much for the sake of the cause. Worse still, organisations and the market can exploit our goodwill. Let me give you an example from a slightly unexpected, small sector: zoos.

Zookeepers love animals but not always their employers

Zookeepers are a niche group of people, and they certainly love animals. So much so that most of them start out as volunteers at zoos and get paid roles only after they have shown their commitment. They see caring for the animals as their calling, which means that many of their employers know their employees will do almost anything for them. This results in a low-pay, long-hours culture, where employees frequently sacrifice their own wellbeing for that of the animals.

I am indebted to Andrew Soren of Eudaimonic by Design for introducing me to a rather brilliant 2009 study (Bunderson and Thompson, 2009) in which researchers found that:

- 91% of zookeepers felt their jobs were a calling
- They often tolerated their own mistreatment because of their deep moral commitment to the animals
- Many worked additional jobs to make ends meet

I shared this research recently and someone replied that she'd worked in a zoo when younger and instantly identified with it. She and her colleagues used to joke, 'We work with monkeys, but we're paid peanuts.'

While zookeeping is quite niche and perhaps suffers more than most, these issues can also arise from working in sectors such as education and healthcare.

Worthwhile work but unfair pay

I can see these patterns clearly in my data. Below is a table comparing three sectors – health, education and charity – in regard to the percentage of people who feel their work is worthwhile, and whether they consider they are paid fairly and report being happy at work.

Meaning and fairness in the UK

	Worthwhile	Fair pay	Happy
UK average	60%	46%	63%
Healthcare	87%	38%	64%
Education	81%	30%	54%
Charity	94%	30%	64%

Note: In my surveys I use the word *worthwhile* to capture the concept of meaningful work.

This data comes from my 2023 survey of the UK working population. It is clear that employment in all three of these sectors is, to varying degrees, high-meaning and of low fairness. Except for the education sector, employees are not unhappy per se, but the intrinsic satisfaction they get from their work is offset by feeling unfairly rewarded. (It's worth noting, though, that 2023 was a particularly fraught time in the UK education sector due to national pay strikes.)

There is clearly a financial penalty for doing meaningful work – a penalty that could be called *meaning discount*. There is also a gender inequality angle on this. Using data from the much larger global study I did in 2016, I can see this gender inequality clearly in the healthcare data.[39] You can see from the table below that the meaning discount is larger for women than for men.

Meaning and fairness by gender in healthcare (global)

	Worthwhile	Fair pay	Happy
Female (healthcare)	84%	50%	71% (n/s)
Male (healthcare)	81%	56%	69% (n/s)

n/s: happiness differences are not statistically significant

---

39 Men are overrepresented in more senior positions, but this only explains part of the effect. The global survey was over 24,000 people from eight nations, of which 2,743 worked in healthcare, so it is a large enough sample to test for statistical significance. The difference in happiness is not statistically significant.

This is evidence of organisations' – and of the market's – tendency to exploit people's desire to do good. Many of the zookeepers were fully aware of this, with one commenting: 'They know you'll do the work, so why [should they] go the extra mile for better pay or conditions?' Another knew this had come at a personal cost: 'Working here cost me my marriage.'

It's wonderful that people are motivated by doing good, but for that motivation to be sustainable, employees also need to be treated well. Otherwise, they're at risk of burning out. My data shows that people in high-meaning jobs who experience low levels of fairness are three times more likely to suffer from burnout than those in equally meaningful roles where they are treated fairly.

Ultimately meaning matters, but it's not enough. If we truly want people to thrive in meaningful work, we must match purpose with fairness. When we don't, we risk turning good intentions into quiet exploitation.

Summary

- **Meaning calls us.** Seeing your work as a calling brings energy, commitment and a deep sense of purpose, and is a powerful source of happiness at work.

- **Meaningful roles are often undervalued.** Many sectors rely on people's passion to justify low pay and tough conditions, leading to a meaning discount.

- **Fairness still matters.** When people are treated fairly, meaningful work becomes truly sustainable. Without it, the risk of burnout rises sharply.

36
Humans, Not Resources

The phrase *Our people are our greatest asset* used to be quoted by senior executives, no doubt with varying levels of sincerity. There can be unintended consequences of thinking of people as assets, though. It's clearly a financial analogy, so I understand why it is appealing, although I am not even sure that seeing people as assets is the right financial analogy. Other assets can't hand in their resignation and leave.

Organisations don't own their people; they rent them

I know it's weird to think of organisations renting rather than owning their employees, but bear with me. The key difference between ownership and a rental agreement is that the latter is about mutuality – both parties need to get value from the relationship. In the case of a property, the landlord receives payment in rent; in return, the tenant gets a space to live in. Because organisations are more powerful than employees, it is easy to instinctively think of the company as the landlord. In fact, though, it is the employee that has something to sell: their *time* and *effort*. Somewhat surprisingly, this analogy flips the traditional power dynamic.

Rental agreements also have trust built into them, as both parties have to deliver on their obligations. There can be issues, of course, just as there are with employment contracts, and the real challenge is not the *time* element but the element of *effort*. Time can be measured and even controlled, but effort is much trickier to pin down. The temptation for organisations, when they view employees as assets that are owned, is to try and control them by squeezing as much effort out of them as possible. The property rental analogy, however, illuminates the inherent reciprocity of the relationship, which is often overlooked.

Analogies are never perfect, but they can be helpful.[40] Just as a tenant reasonably expects their landlord to maintain the property, it's fair for an employer to

---

40 The seminal book *Images of Organization* (Morgan, 1986) is an excellent read about how metaphors can help us understand organisational systems and dynamics.

expect a reasonable level of effort from their employees. This is why reciprocity, alignment and fairness are essential foundations for building happy, successful teams.

From human resources to resourceful humans

The shift from viewing an organisation as renting an employee's time rather than owning them shows the power of reframing and highlights how the metaphors we choose often carry deeper assumptions than we initially realise. Referring to the people function in an organisation as the 'HR department' can also suffer from unintended consequences. Let me explain more.

HR departments started to gain prominence in the mid twentieth century, replacing what were often called personnel departments. It was part of a shift in the function becoming more strategic and not purely administrative. The idea was that employees were a critical resource and a valuable asset to organisations, and that this should be reflected in the title of the department managing them.

We are so used to the term HR that we barely think what it means, but it does again imply employees are assets, that humans are resources for the organisation. Instead of human resources, let's talk about *resourceful humans*. Also, let's not keep these resourceful humans within a separate department but instead distribute them throughout all the teams in the whole organisation.

This neat linguistic switch, from human resources to resourceful humans, is more than a metaphor. It is a change in how the people-management function in an organisation works. Many companies have already renamed their HR directors as people directors, and others have created HR partners that sit in the departments they are responsible for. Resourceful humans outside of a department suggests going even further, though, as it emphasises the need to distribute resourcefulness throughout the organisation.

It's important not to throw the baby out with the bathwater (to use another metaphor). HR departments play a vital role, especially as organisations grow. They help build fair structures and efficient systems, preventing people-management issues that can derail scaling companies. Fairness must also extend to how promotions and rewards are handled, which requires clear systems and transparency. When those systems become overly rigid or bureaucratic, though, they can stifle teams instead of supporting them, which undermines agility and innovation.

It can be hard to strike the right balance between organised systems and overbearing control. However, a focus on team happiness helps. It is precisely the same tension that two different types of happiness help us navigate: the twin, but frequently conflicting, needs to maintain stability and drive positive change.

Ultimately, the language and metaphors we use shape how we think about and interact with people in organisations. By moving beyond outdated approaches, where employees are talked of as assets and resources, we can create a more empowering language that reflects the mutuality, autonomy and creativity of modern workplaces.

Summary

- **People are not possessions.** Thinking of employees as assets to be owned misses the point – people can walk away. Trust and reciprocity flourish when we recognise employment as a mutual exchange, not control.

- **Organisations need to flip the power dynamic.** If effort is what's truly being rented, then it's employees who hold the keys. Fairness, alignment and respect are the real drivers of sustainable commitment.

- **Language matters.** Reframing HR from 'human resources' to 'resourceful humans' encourages a culture of shared responsibility and distributed leadership.

37
Why Employee Engagement Doesn't Add Up

If you are a team or senior leader, employee engagement sounds a great idea. Let's be honest, though – it's just a codeword for productivity. In fact, the use of the word *engagement* in the work context is recent; it was first coined in 1990 by Boston University's William Kahn (Kahn, 1990). It was rapidly picked up by management consultancies, who saw it as a proxy for employees' discretionary effort, meaning that both time and effort could now be measured. It's easy to understand why those consultants were so excited.

Gallup, who have probably championed the term the most, still say that only 23% of the workforce are 'actively engaged'. They estimate that $8.9 trillion is lost in potential global GDP as a result (Gallup, 2024). Yes, $8.9 trillion! That's roughly double Germany's total annual GDP. Then there are all the hundreds of billions that are spent trying to boost engagement, which clearly haven't been very effective.[41]

Perhaps it is time for a rethink.

What does engagement really mean?

There are as many definitions of engagement as there are consultancies selling engagement solutions. Think about it this way – could you answer the following question: *How engaged are you at work?*

Maybe you could – that you are reading this book likely means you understand more than most what is meant by engagement. What about most workers, though? Could a truck driver answer it? A teacher? A trainee?

Engagement is simply not a word that is used in everyday conversation; it is more corporate speak. Also, what would it take to be *fully* engaged? Would you have to be 100% focused all of the time? Available on call 24/7?

In contrast, consider this question: *How happy are you at work?*

---

41 It's hard to put a figure on expenditure on employee engagement, but global expenditure on training is over $350 billion, so it certainly is about that order of magnitude different. I always have to remind myself just how big a number a trillion is, ie one thousand billion.

Suddenly, everyone has an answer. Everyone knows how happy they are, as happiness is part of our human nature. We understand the top of the scale too, as happiness naturally has balance built into it, whereas if we try and focus 100% for too long, we become exhausted and unhappy.

The problem with how engagement is measured

Let's now consider the second issue I have with engagement: how it can be measured.

In Chapter 40 I'll introduce you to my Dynamic Model of Team Happiness, which shows the relationship between the Five Ways and the Seven Successes of Happy Teams. This gives a clear distinction between outcomes and drivers, and they are measured independently of each other, which enables the relationship between them to be statistically investigated.

This kind of analysis is not possible with most engagement surveys. Take Gallup's approach, for example. Engagement is measured with what has become known as their *Q12* – twelve questions that they claim together measure engagement. Those questions are all drivers, though there is no outcome measure. The Q12 is subject to copyright and so can't be reproduced here, which is fair enough, but Gallup are elusive about how they define 'engaged'.[42]

I suspect Gallup create an engagement score by adding up all the responses. Then they probably create a cut-off and categorise a high score as being 'highly engaged'. While calculating and presenting scores like this is good marketing for Gallup's consultancy services, it isn't great statistics. The groupings are inevitably somewhat arbitrary. However, there is a bigger statistical crime! There is a hidden assumption that all twelve drivers have an equal impact on the unmeasured (and probably unmeasurable) construct of engagement. For example, one of the Q12 questions is about having a best friend at work while another is about using your strengths. Are they both equally powerful drivers of engagement? I don't know, but I do know it should be an empirical question. You can only answer this question if you have an independent outcome variable. This is the technique I used earlier, when I showed that boredom undermined happiness at work four times more than stress. I had the data to be able to compare the strength of the impact.

When I explore drivers of happiness at work, I know that different drivers have different weights of impact. Not only that, but the weights can also

---

42 This is a direct quote from one of their latest reports (Gallup, 2024): 'Gallup's proprietary formula does not require perfect agreement with all Q12 elements for employees to be classified as engaged.'

vary depending on the context. Let me give you an example.

Accountants need love, and advertisers want meaning

In 2017 I collaborated with the global recruitment agency Robert Half on a large international survey of over 22,000 workers, conducted as part of their research into how to 'work happy'. The survey included the fifteen questions that now form the basis of my Five Ways questionnaire, making it a crucial step in the development and selection of those items. While all fifteen questions proved to be strong drivers of happiness, they didn't all carry equal weight. Typically, the top three were 'accomplishment', 'appreciation' and 'organisational pride'. Thanks to the size of the dataset, I was also able to explore how the relative influence of these factors varied across different sectors.

After the survey was released, I did several talks for Robert Half's clients. I now somewhat playfully say, *Accountants need love, and advertisers want meaning*. This is because the data showed that the difference between the happiest and the least happy accountants was best explained by how appreciated they felt. For advertisers, meanwhile, most important was having work they felt was worthwhile. The key point is that different drivers will have different weights, and they will vary according to the context. You can only evaluate this if you have different measures for outcomes and drivers.

Happiness is more engaging than engagement

All this means that employee engagement isn't a well-defined concept, and it can't be measured directly. What does it really mean when Gallup claim that only 23% of the global workforce are engaged? The significance is unclear, and with all due respect, that conclusion seems disrespectful to the global workforce, with the majority defined as not engaged.

This is the nub of my third issue with employee engagement, especially when it comes to creating a positive, productive culture at work. Engagement is so obviously the organisation's agenda. What is in it for the employee to become more engaged? This is possibly about the future prospect of bonuses or promotion, but it's not talking about anything immediate or anything about their actual experience of work. Happiness, on the other hand, is an entirely different proposition – it is very much connected to our internal reward system and our motivation.

Somewhat ironically, happiness is more engaging than engagement!

Summary

- **Engagement is vague; happiness is human.** Despite its popularity, 'engagement' is corporate jargon that lacks clear meaning for most employees. In contrast, everyone knows how happy they feel at work, making happiness a far more intuitive and useful concept.

- **Happiness can be poorly measured and misunderstood.** Engagement surveys, like Gallup's Q12, rely on driver-only questions and fuzzy thresholds to classify workers, but they offer no independent outcome measure. Without distinguishing between causes and effects, we can't know what truly matters.

- **There is a better way forward.** Happiness provides a more grounded, motivating and measurable approach. It aligns business outcomes with employee experience and allows leaders to discover which drivers matter most in their specific context.

38
Annual Surveys Aren't The Answer

Surveys play a vital role in understanding how people are feeling at work. Done well, they can reveal what's working, what's not and where there's room to improve – both for teams and the wider organisation. Surveys only matter if they lead to action, though. In this chapter I'll explore why shorter, more regular pulse surveys are often more effective – not just because they offer more timely data, but also because they make it easier to turn insight into meaningful change.

The first thing to note is that 52% of workers in my 2023 representative survey said they hadn't been given the opportunity to complete a staff survey in the past two years, as shown below.

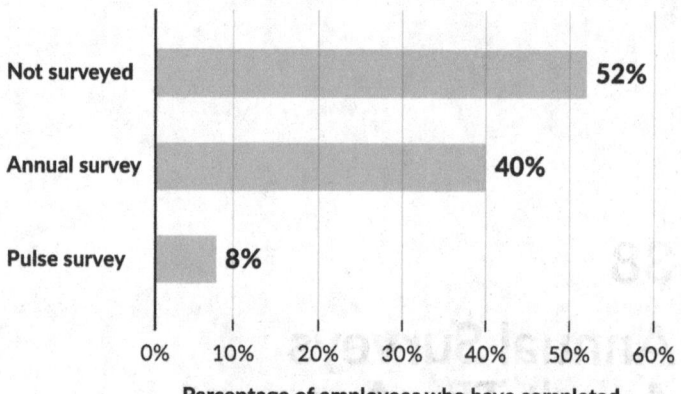

Survey participation by type

The chart below shows that people working in organisations that don't run staff surveys are significantly less happy than those who do. That's not to say the surveys themselves are the direct cause – correlation isn't causation. Rather, it suggests that organisations which run surveys tend to be better places to work overall, likely because they have practices in place, such as actively seeking employee feedback, that support better ways of working.

Doing an annual staff survey is of course better than not doing a survey at all. If it is well conducted and followed up, an annual survey can both help improve the experience of working in the organisation and drive business success. However, pulse surveys, which I define as quarterly or more frequent, are significantly better.

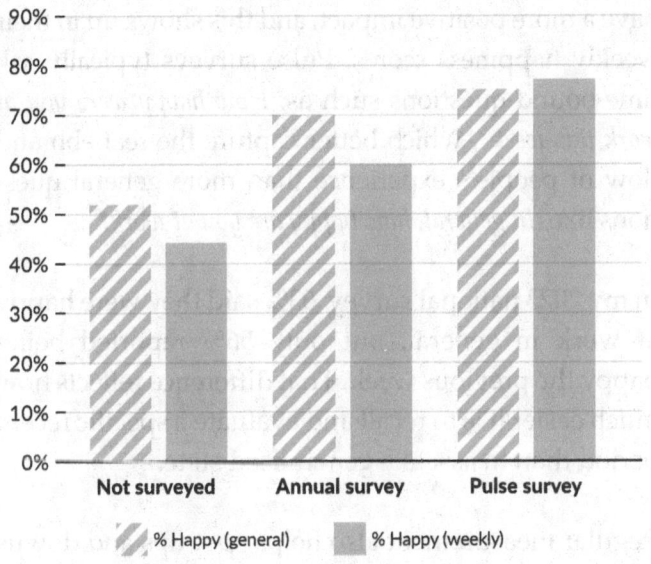

Impact of annual and pulse surveys on employee happiness

Above is a chart reflecting the impact of annual and pulse surveys on people's experience of work, with statistics from a representative UK sample of 1,500 employees on a survey I conducted in 2023. The annual group includes all non-pulse surveys, which are predominantly annual but include also six-monthly, biannual and non-regular surveys (but in the two years prior to the date of the survey).

Pulse surveys make more impact

Although only a small percentage of organisations currently use pulse surveys, employees report that they have a more positive impact; and this shows up in their weekly happiness scores. Pulse surveys typically ask time-bound questions such as, *How happy were you at work this week?*, which better capture the real ebb and flow of people's experience than more general questions like, *In general, how happy are you at work?*

In my 2023 national survey, 63% said they were happy at work in general, but only 56% reported being happy the previous week. That difference reflects how much easier it is to recall and evaluate a specific recent period than to assess a generalised state.

Regular measurement also helps spot ups and downs in team experience. Think back to the graph I shared in Chapter 1, showing weekly happiness during the first months of the pandemic – only regular measurement can reveal those trendlines. In the workplace that kind of tracking can serve as an early warning system for team leaders.

These are the key reasons that annual staff surveys are no longer fit for purpose. Pulse surveys are the future – they produce more nuanced insights, more timely data and ultimately more effective action.

Summary

- **Shorter timeframes yield better data.** People recall recent experiences far more accurately than general ones, so weekly questions generate more meaningful insights than annual surveys ever can.

- **Pulse surveys track the real ups and downs.** They capture the natural rhythm of working life – its highs, lows and turning points – in a way annual check-ins simply can't.

- **Regular feedback drives real change.** More frequent data not only reflects reality more clearly; it also builds momentum for timely, practical action.

39
What Hunter-Gatherers Teach Us About Questionnaire Design

From the charioteer of Plato's dialogues to the three Greek gods of time, we've seen how ancient insights can help us think differently about modern challenges. In this short chapter I want to go back even further – to a time before writing and civilisation, when small groups of humans roamed and survived as hunter-gatherers. What could their ways of thinking possibly teach us about survey design? As it turns out, quite a lot – especially about the power of five.

Ancient hunter-gatherer tribes might seem a strange source of wisdom for designing modern pulse surveys, but there is something very interesting about their use of numbers: they had words only for numbers up to four or five. After that, they used words such as *many* or *more*. This highlights something we might not be aware of – that we, as all humans, can't instantly count groups of objects with more than about four or five items in them. After that, we estimate. For a wonderful exploration of this and many other mathematical oddities, see *Alex's Adventures in Numberland* (Bellos, 2010).

Humans can only count to five (without counting)

Think of it this way. In your kitchen you might have a bowl of fruit. If there were four lemons in it, you could instantly look and identify the number. If, though, there were eight lemons, you wouldn't instantly know how many there were. To be precise, you would have to individually count them.

We see the same effect with counting tallies. We will happily put four vertical lines when counting this way and then strike those out to make a bundle of five, as illustrated below.

Counting in fives

Roman numerals used a similar system, with V (5) being the second smallest unit. They predominantly used IV for the number 4, but if you look at the faces of most watches and clocks with Roman numerals, you will notice that they have reverted back to the more ancient IIII for 4 o'clock. That's because it is instinctively easier to read than the IV.

Questionnaire designers should take notice

What does this all have to do with questionnaire design? The answer is response codes.

Many questionnaires use a 0–10 scale for you to give your answer. It feels a natural scale to use, as we have ten fingers, and our number system is base-10. However, it is quite hard to know how to gauge responses. People start pondering whether they should answer, say, with 7 or 8. This problem gets amplified when answering a whole battery of similarly formatted questions. In tests where a researcher observes someone filling in a questionnaire, they often report that respondents get confused, slow down and even sometimes go back and change previous answers. Although a 0–10 point scale looks and feels natural, it isn't really intuitive for us to use.

Five is an odd number, which is an advantage

When I design questionnaires, I always use a five-point scale, which has the advantage of being an odd number because there is a middle button. This is important because sometimes the respondent wants to answer 'somewhere in the middle'. If faced with an even number of response codes, they are forced into giving a positive or negative reply. I know why researchers like this – they can then categorise responses in two neat buckets: positive and negative, happy and unhappy, etc. As soon as the responder feels pushed one way or another, though, some nuance to the data has been lost. It's much better to allow responders the middle option, which I label as 'OK' in my happiness questions. In the analysis I then look at how the OKs *differ* from the happy and the unhappy.

There are a couple of other advantages to a five-point scale, especially in comparison with longer ones:

- Five-point scales display better on smaller electronic devices, making it less likely that people will accidentally tap the wrong option.
- For visually oriented users, colour-coded traffic light systems work well, but the more response options you have, the harder it is to distinguish subtle shades of red, yellow and green.
- It's also easier to label five response categories clearly – for example: *very unhappy, unhappy, OK, happy, very happy*. With seven options the language becomes more awkward and less intuitive.

When presenting results, I often simplify the five-point scale into three groups: *unhappy, OK* and *happy*. This makes it easier to interpret graphs at a glance while still retaining the nuance of the middle category. It also highlights an important insight: OK often isn't OK.

Summary

- **We're wired for small sets.** Our brains are remarkably good at recognising small quantities without counting – usually up to four or five. Beyond that, we estimate. That simple truth has deep implications for how we process information.

- **Odd numbers offer balance.** A five-point scale lets people choose the middle – neither positive nor negative – which is critical for capturing nuance. With even-numbered scales, nuance gets forced out.

- **Five is a human number.** The number five is easy to display, easy to label and fits how we naturally think. That's why five-point scales tend to work better – for researchers, for respondents and for clearer results.

PART SIX
BUILDING HAPPY TEAMS

40
Introducing The Dynamic Model Of Team Happiness

It's time to introduce the core model behind this book. I think of models as maps – they help us make sense of complex terrain and guide us as we navigate it. When it comes to team happiness, the terrain is both complex and constantly shifting.

This isn't the first time I've worked on a dynamic model like this. Alongside my colleague Dr Sam Thompson, I developed an earlier version for the UK Government Office of Science back in 2008 (Marks and Thompson, 2008). That original model was designed to understand personal wellbeing, but its core ideas have stood the test of time. This new version builds on that foundation and applies it specifically to teams.

Of course, any model is a simplification. The challenge is to distil complexity without losing meaning. What I've aimed for here is a model that's as simple as possible without being simplistic. The simplicity has been hard-won, shaped and tested through years of research and practical application.

At the heart of the model is a simple but powerful truth: happy teams are successful teams. The Dynamic Model of Team Happiness shows how and why that's the case – and what you can do to make it happen.

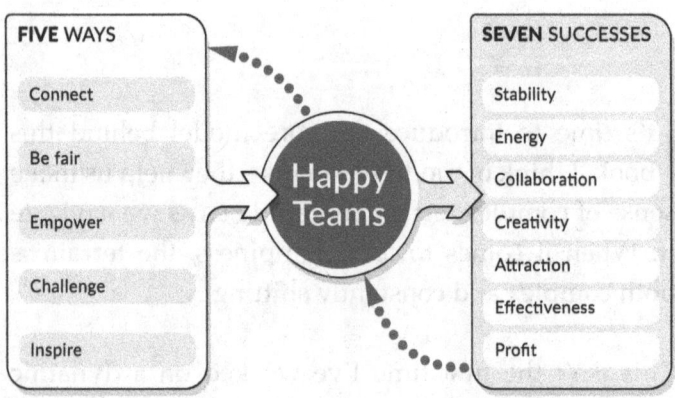

The Dynamic Model of Team Happiness

Happy Teams are at the centre of the model. How to build happy teams is the focus of this part of the book and indeed the aim of this whole book.

The Five Ways on the left are the main drivers of happiness at work.

The Seven Successes on the right are the positive impacts of team happiness.

Most of the energy in the system flows from left to right, capturing the dynamic nature of happiness. However, teams and organisations are complex living systems, in which cause and effect are entwined.

The dynamic flow of energy

The arrows flowing from left to right indicate the primary causal pathway. The Five Ways build happy teams, which leads to the Seven Successes. In this way, team happiness is both a valuable outcome and a driver of business success.

The model can also be read from right to left. From this perspective, success is what drives happiness. Hard work leads to success, which in turn brings happiness. This is reflected in lighter arrows in the model, but they are deliberately less prominent. Studies tracking team happiness and performance have found that the effect of happiness on success is about twice as strong as the effect of success on happiness. In other words, while success can make people happier, happiness is a much stronger driver of success.[43]

---

[43] In a classic paper (Harter et al, 2010), the chief wellbeing scientist at Gallup summarised his findings: 'These data suggest that the impact of work perceptions on financial performance is about twice as large as the impact of financial performance on work perceptions.'

There is also an arrow from happy teams back to the Five Ways. This highlights that happier teams also work better together, reinforcing the very drivers that made them happy in the first place.

Two virtuous cycles

The model reveals two virtuous cycles that reinforce why happiness is a serious business:

1. Team happiness and business success
2. Strong team functioning and happiness

1. Team happiness and business success

In this first virtuous cycle, team happiness leads to business success, which in turn generates more team happiness.

This self-reinforcing pattern is why organisations that invest in happiness thrive, while those that neglect it risk falling into decline.

Just as there is a positive loop, there is also a risk of a downward spiral. Unhappy teams are less effective, which leads to weaker business results, which in turn further undermines happiness. This cycle can contribute to underperformance, flight and burnout.

2. Strong team functioning and happiness

This second virtuous cycle happens on the left side of the model. Strong team functioning leads to happiness, which then strengthens team functioning even further.

This is where interventions can make the biggest difference. Happy teams do not just happen. They emerge from positive working relationships, behaviours and habits. Supporting teams in this way opens up the pathway to sustainable happiness and performance.

In contrast, teams that struggle with poor relationships, weak leadership or dysfunctional habits can quickly decline. Many of the stories from Part Four of this book illustrate this downward cycle in action.

The two feedback loops as learning opportunities

The two virtuous cycles in the dynamic model offer powerful learning opportunities, which systems thinkers and engineers call positive or reinforcing feedback loops.[44] The word *positive* in this context does

---

44 I have been heavily influenced by multiple systems thinkers over the years. If I had to pick one particular one, it would be Stafford Beer, who was an original thinker and rather marvellously, with his long hair and beard, looked like an Old Testament prophet. The field he worked in at the time was called cybernetics, which was founded by Norbert Wiener in 1948 (Beer, 1981). Among many other innovations, it explored how systems regulate themselves through feedback mechanisms. It has been highly influential in AI development.

not mean good – it simply means the effect amplifies itself. Like a microphone feeding back into a speaker, this can be helpful or harmful.

If the signal being amplified is happiness, there is potential for compounding positive effects. My approach is specifically designed to harness these loops for team learning.

HI (happiness intelligence)

The approach I propose later is designed to amplify these two virtuous cycles, using a measurement-led process that enables teams and leaders to track their own growth. At its core, happiness is an internal signal, indicating whether things are going well or badly. Every team member is like a sensor, and their feelings provide valuable data about how the team is functioning.

To get a bit nerdy for a second: this is a Bayesian process – a statistical approach that helps us make better decisions in the face of uncertainty. Instead of starting from scratch each time, we adjust what we believe based on what we experience. It's a bit like updating your internal map of the world whenever new information comes in. Named after eighteenth-century minister Thomas Bayes, who was a statistician in his spare time, this method is often called scientific common sense because it mirrors how we naturally learn and adapt in real life (Chivers, 2024).

AI and machine learning tools follow a similar logic, continually refining their models based on incoming data. Many neuroscientists also take a Bayesian approach in understanding how perception and consciousness work, suggesting that the brain itself functions as a kind of prediction engine, constantly updating its understanding of reality (Seth, 2021).

The process I introduce in the next chapter follows this same logic, except it uses HI to help teams and organisations understand their current situation better and self-correct and adapt dynamically.

The bigger picture: Team happiness in a dynamic system

Happiness is not just contained within a team. Its effects ripple out across an organisation, shaping staff turnover, burnout, customer sales, innovation, talent attraction, productivity and even share price growth. Many of the cautionary tales I've shared in this book illustrate how changes in one area can have unexpected effects elsewhere.

The Dynamic Model of Team Happiness provides a framework for understanding these complex interactions. It is deceptively simple, yet it captures a great deal of underlying complexity. It shows that happiness is both a result of good team functioning and a driver of success. The energy also flows in reverse, with success influencing happiness, which then reshapes the team environment.

Ripple effects and unintended consequences

In a complex system, no factor operates in isolation. Improvements in one area can ripple outward, while neglect in another can lead to cascading problems. Some interventions solve one issue but create problems elsewhere.

This is why the dynamic model is so useful. It allows us to step back and see the whole system, helping us anticipate unintended consequences. For example, introducing flexible working might improve wellbeing, but it can also weaken team cohesion if not carefully managed. This is a real dilemma that I have touched on before and will return to later.

Where to intervene

Organisations and teams are interconnected systems, so there are many points where interventions can be made. In my model, team happiness sits at the centre, making it natural for us to focus on its drivers and impacts. Other models may place business outcomes such as productivity at their core, but any truly holistic approach must still account for all these interconnecting factors like relationships, wellbeing and purpose.

Interventions that focus directly on business outcomes like productivity can also be risky if team happiness is neglected. While success can boost happiness, the pathway from success to happiness is much weaker than the pathway from happiness to success. This helps explain why high-performing teams that aren't happy often experience elevated levels of burnout and staff turnover. In the happiness × performance quadrant I shared in Chapter 22, unhappy high-performing teams had three times higher rates of both compared to happy high-performing teams.

I will go into more detail about interventions later, but I would go as far as to say that focusing exclusively on improving performance rarely creates happy teams, but investing in team happiness almost always improves performance.

Measuring the impact of interventions

The failure of many wellbeing programmes is not just disappointing; it is revealing. Many initiatives fail simply because their impact is not measured properly. The Dynamic Model of Team Happiness highlights three areas that must be tracked separately to understand real impact:

1. **Drivers of happiness** (such as team behaviours and interactions)
2. **Happiness itself** (team experience)
3. **Success outcomes** (performance indicators)

If these are not tracked independently, their interrelationships remain murky. This is why I have critiqued certain measures like Gallup's Q12, which blends drivers and outcomes, making it hard to see what is actually influencing what.

Some measures are also mislabelled. eNPS, for example, is often used as a proxy for employee experience, but it's better understood – through the lens of the Dynamic Model – as an outcome measure, specifically reflecting the attraction element of the Seven Successes. Similarly, work–life balance is sometimes used as a proxy for happiness, but in the Dynamic Model, it is more accurately seen as a driver – part of fairness within the Five Ways. That said, it's arguably less misleading than eNPS, as it reflects the employee's experience rather than the employer's agenda. Getting the classification right matters. When we blur the lines, we risk drawing the wrong conclusions and missing the opportunity to make real change.

The Dynamic Model of Team Happiness helps uncover the hidden forces that shape team success. By showing how happiness is both a driver and an outcome, the model offers leaders a clear, practical framework for building teams that thrive. In the next chapter I introduce a method to bring this model to life, turning insight into action and helping teams move from intention to impact.

Summary

- **Happiness drives success more than success drives happiness.** The Dynamic Model of Team Happiness reveals that, while success can influence happiness, it's happiness that has the stronger impact on team performance – about twice as strong. Investing in team happiness creates a virtuous cycle of improved functioning and sustained success.

- **Teams are dynamic systems with feedback loops.** The model highlights two key reinforcing cycles: one between team functioning and happiness, and another between happiness and business outcomes. Like all systems, these loops can spiral up or down, so timely, targeted support is essential to maintain positive momentum.

- **We need to measure what matters, separately.** To understand the real impact of any intervention, it's vital to track drivers, outcomes and team happiness as distinct variables. When we blur these, as some surveys do, we lose clarity. The Dynamic Model helps us step back, see the system and intervene more wisely.

41
Simple, Three-Step Process For Building Happy Teams

Over the last two decades, I have worked with thousands of teams, helping them measure and improve their happiness at work. My initial attempts were undeniably overcomplicated, as I had yet to fully grasp the power of simplicity. Through years of refinement, I've distilled the process of collecting and acting on HI (happiness intelligence) down to three simple steps:

1. **Measure.** Well-designed pulse checks and surveys generate HI metrics that are relevant, responsive and actionable. Having clear data helps leaders take their people's experience at work seriously.

2. **Meet.** Measurement alone achieves nothing unless it leads to action. I recommend that

teams meet regularly to discuss their results, as how teams function together is a major driver of happiness. These discussions empower teams, fostering self-awareness and naturally motivating them to improve how they work together.

3. **Repeat.** Maintaining momentum is critical to any change process, and regularly repeating these steps ensures that team development remains a consistent priority.

Measure-meet-repeat – I told you it was simple. The key is that this is a repeated pattern, as illustrated in the diagram below. It is also a continuous learning process, which over time deepens everyone's understanding of what makes for good work – work that is both enjoyable and valuable.

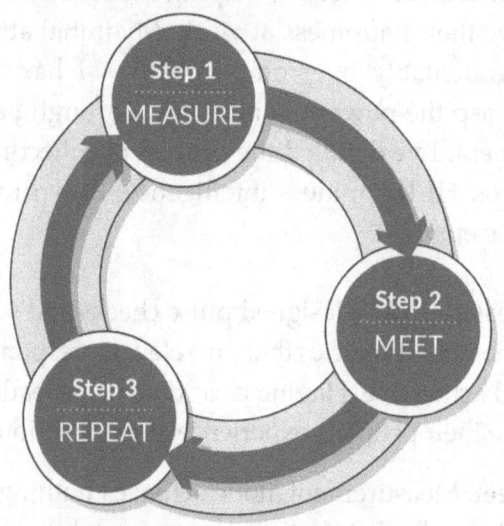

Measure-meet-repeat cycle

SIMPLE, THREE-STEP PROCESS FOR BUILDING HAPPY TEAMS

Two speeds, one system

As covered in Chapter 40, there are two interconnected feedback cycles in the Dynamic Model of Team Happiness:

1. Functional teams lead to happiness, which in turn strengthens team functioning.

2. Team happiness leads to success, which in turn generates more happiness.

Measure-meet-repeat brings both of these cycles to life, though at different speeds. The first cycle is slower and deeper, while the second is faster and lighter. Both cycles are powered by happiness data, allowing teams to learn how to become both happier and more successful.

Slower, deeper cycle: The Five Ways pulse survey

The left side of the Dynamic Model of Team Happiness follows a more traditional learning process, similar to how most staff surveys are conducted. The Five Ways pulse survey is designed to be used quarterly, as follows:

- **Measure** team happiness and its key drivers.
- **Meet** as a team to reflect on the results and decide what to change.
- **Repeat** the process in the next quarter.

299

While the *measure* part of my approach may look similar to a traditional staff survey, what follows represents a meaningful shift. Most surveys are run top-down – data is gathered, analysed centrally and then interpreted by leaders or HR, with actions often decided far from the teams themselves.

Measure-meet-repeat flips this dynamic. By reviewing their own data regularly, teams are encouraged to take ownership of their experience and how they work together. It's a more participatory and empowering process – one that recognises the team as the most immediate and influential setting for people's day-to-day working lives. Rather than waiting for top-down solutions, it enables real change from the inside out.

Faster, lighter cycle: The happiness pulse check

The right side of the Dynamic Model of Team Happiness follows a faster feedback loop between team happiness and success. This is where a weekly or monthly happiness pulse check can be particularly valuable. The process remains the same but operates on a more immediate timeline:

- **Measure** team happiness weekly (or monthly)
- **Meet** as a team to reflect on the past week (or month), building on positives and addressing frustrations
- **Repeat** the process at the next check-in

I prefer the weekly cadence because most teams work in weekly cycles. It also ensures that teams regularly pay attention to how they are working together. However, many organisations I have worked with find that a monthly rhythm suits their needs.

To avoid cumbersome phrasing, I will refer to this faster cycle as the *weekly pulse check* throughout the rest of this book.

Measure-meet-repeat is a simple but powerful process that helps teams work better together and stay happy while doing it. It is easy to adopt, and over time it builds a habit of paying attention to what really matters. By maintaining this rhythm, teams can learn, adapt and improve in a way that feels natural rather than forced. It is not about ticking boxes – it is about making happiness and success part of everyday team life.

While the process is elegantly simple, it still needs some unpacking to be put into practice. The next chapter breaks down each stage of measure-meet-repeat and provides all the guidance you'll need to bring it to life in your team or organisation.

Summary

- **The measure-meet-repeat process is simple but powerful.** Measure-meet-repeat provides a rhythm that helps teams use HI to improve both how they work and how they feel, building habits that support growth, learning and success.
- **Change needs to be team-led.** Unlike traditional, top-down surveys, this approach puts insight and responsibility in the hands of the team, creating a more participatory, empowering process that drives real improvement from the inside out.

42
Measure-Meet-Repeat In More Detail

Whether you're leading a single team or shaping the direction of an entire organisation, this chapter provides practical guidance on how to bring the measure-meet-repeat process to life. It breaks down each stage, offering simple, actionable steps to help build a rhythm of reflection, dialogue and improvement – one that keeps both happiness and performance front of mind.

1. Measure: Tracking and understanding team happiness

If you want to build a great team culture, measurement is essential. Without it, you are working in the dark.

As a reminder: the two different cycles introduced in the previous chapter need different but complementary measurement tools:

- **The Five Ways pulse survey** – acting like a happiness diagnostic, this helps teams and organisations understand their strengths and areas for improvement. It supports the quarterly deeper learning cycle.

- **The weekly pulse check** – tracking the ups and downs of everyday work, this acts as an early warning system, allowing teams and leaders to respond quickly. It fuels the weekly faster learning cycle.

Each serves a different purpose, but together they create a clear and dynamic picture of team happiness.

Understanding team happiness with a heatmap

Every organisation I have worked with has big differences between teams. Each team has its own challenges, dynamics and personalities, which means no two teams experience work in exactly the same way. To highlight this, it helps to create a heatmap, showing how happiness scores vary across teams.

To make this more relatable, I will use as an example data on happiness in different UK industries rather than an anonymised company version. I have

Five Ways heatmap of UK sectors

	Happiness	Connect			Be fair			Empower			Challenge			Inspire		
		Team relationships	Team cooperation	Friendships at work	Fairness and respect	Appreciation	Work-life balance	Strengths	Freeness to be self	Ability to influence decisions	Creativity	Feedback	Learning	Pride	Worthwhile work	Accomplishment
UK overall	66	80	69	67	69	62	64	67	69	57	54	58	59	66	70	67
Marketing and creative agencies	77	87	81	74	76	73	67	71	69	70	78	72	72	74	72	75
Health and social care	68	81	68	69	70	60	65	69	72	57	53	58	61	71	81	75
Hospitality	68	80	69	69	68	64	66	66	73	60	56	57	59	65	65	64
Technology	66	80	71	67	73	65	65	67	71	60	58	62	63	69	68	66
Professional services	66	82	71	67	71	66	63	68	70	57	52	60	63	67	68	67
Manufacturing	64	78	66	67	67	58	62	65	64	52	50	52	54	60	66	64
Education	63	77	66	68	65	58	53	69	64	53	60	56	56	67	76	71

included seven sectors: the six largest, plus marketing and creative agencies as a point of comparison. These sectors are ranked by happiness, with education coming out as the least happy.

Some patterns stand out immediately, for example:

- Team relationships score highly across all sectors, which is something I have seen in virtually every survey I have conducted.
- Challenge scores lowest across all sectors, particularly in areas like creativity and helpful feedback. One clear takeaway is that improving how leaders give feedback is critical – not just for happiness, but for success too.

Looking at the sector heatmap, and imagining these industries as teams, the education team could learn a lot from the marketing team.

Of course, their challenges are completely different. At the time of this survey, the UK education sector had been through years of neglect, was struggling with low morale, and there was widespread talk of strike action. The heatmap reflects these tensions, highlighting poor work–life balance and lack of appreciation, which is a combination that strongly predicts burnout. Marketing and creative agencies generally score much higher on happiness. Those agencies tend to offer more autonomy, higher appreciation, and a greater sense of creativity and challenge, all of which are key happiness drivers. Of course, this does not mean that the education sector should suddenly adopt everything from marketing, but it does show that some work environments naturally support happiness better than others.

Using the Five Ways as a lens helps uncover why certain sectors – or teams – thrive while others struggle. If you map happiness across your own organisation, you will almost certainly find big variations between teams. Understanding these patterns is the first step towards improving them.

Tracking team happiness over time

Think back to Chapter 1 and the graph of UK happiness during the early stages of the pandemic. It captured the ups and downs of an extraordinary year, showing how quickly moods shifted in response to events. That data came from a weekly happiness measure, and I use a similar approach in my work with teams.

At the end of each week, team members are asked *How happy were you at work this week?* on a five-point scale. We also ask a few open-ended questions about what has gone well and what has been frustrating. The results are then fed back to the team so they can discuss their experience of work in real time.

Over time this data builds a trendline. In the example below, you can see that this team experienced a major setback a couple of months ago, but they have since bounced back into the healthy upper zone.

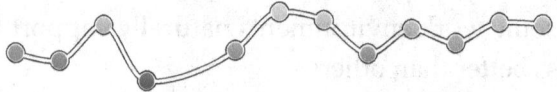

Typical trendline of organisational happiness

This kind of tracking is incredibly useful because happiness naturally fluctuates. Teams can use the data to understand what helps them thrive and what drags them down.

Measurement is just the first step

Measuring team happiness is where the process starts, not where it ends. Data alone does not create change. The real value comes when teams meet to reflect on the results and decide on required actions.

2. Meet: Actions speak louder than numbers

People often use the old adage, *Actions speak louder than words,* and a similar version applies to numbers. Measuring team happiness and its key drivers is a great start, but measurement by itself changes nothing. In fact, asking teams how happy they are and then doing nothing with the results is worse than not asking them at all – you've given them a voice but not listened. Measurement can kickstart the process, but actions speak louder than numbers.

Some of the insights from both the Five Ways pulse survey and the weekly pulse check will be organisation-wide, but many will be particular to certain teams. Teams will also be better than outsiders at understanding the nuances of their results, and they can often take action on their own.

The whole process is, of course, an investment, but one of time rather than cash. It's worth always remembering that happy employees add twice as much value as OK ones. Nudging teams towards happier ways of working is therefore a great return on investment.

Invest a little time every week

The weekly data can make a start-the-week meeting much more effective. It encourages the team to reflect on the previous week, especially on what they have achieved. Too often teams rush from one challenge to another without even pausing to see what they have accomplished. Collecting and discussing data provides such a simple way of appreciating everyone's efforts. Teams then build on these positives and, if necessary, tackle any frustrations.

I recommend this meeting is held at the same time every week. A simple agenda is as follows:

- Celebrate and build on everyone's achievements (increase flow)
- Surface and tackle any frustrations people have (reduce friction)
- Agree any actions

These meetings don't need to be long. Just ten to fifteen minutes a week will reap a lot of benefits.

Once a quarter, take a little longer

The quarterly pulse survey is a deeper dive into how teams work together. As the example above on different sectors in the UK showed, such a survey can provide very actionable insights.

I always encourage teams to set aside one to two hours to reflect on their results and decide what actions they are going to take, which can form a great segment of a quarterly gathering or away day. This is especially true for teams that don't work together at the same location.

The agenda for such a meeting is straightforward:

- Start with the positives:
    - Identify scores you are proud of.
    - Discuss what's behind them.
    - Celebrate them, and think how you can maintain them.

- Recognise your challenges:
  - Identify any lower scores.
  - Choose one, or maximum two, challenges to focus on.
  - Break into small groups to discuss what's holding people back.

- Identify actions to take:
  - Create a picture of what 'good' would look like.
  - Consider what you could do differently (that is under your control).
  - Think about what support or resources you need.

- Follow up and follow through:
  - Make a plan, and implement changes.
  - Review progress towards the 'good'.
  - Make adjustments if needed.

This simple methodology, of building on positives and tackling negatives, has been the core of my work for organisations for the last decade.

3. Repeat: Excellence is a habit

This final section focuses on the need to keep repeating this cycle and demonstrates how transformative it can be as a process.

'Excellence is a habit' – a quote from Aristotle – highlights the best way to become excellent at building happy, successful teams. Measure-meet-repeat is a measurement-led way of helping teams and organisations achieve this.

In his best-selling book *Atomic Habits,* James Clear defines a habit as 'a routine or a behaviour that is performed regularly' (Clear, 2018). He goes on to explain why habits are so powerful:

> 'Habits are the compound interest of self-improvement. The same way that money multiplies through compound interest, the effects of your habits multiple as you repeat them. They seem to make little difference on any given day, and yet the impact they deliver over months and years can be enormous.'

Repeatedly measuring and then meeting is precisely how the compound interest of the successes that flow from team happiness is accumulated. Healthy processes and habits are why happy teams are successful teams, and how companies create a happiness dividend that generates 3% extra share price growth.

Team happiness builds slowly but surely

One team leader was appointed to turn around an unhappy team. He committed to the measure-meet-repeat methodology, and over time he rebuilt trust and the team started to work better together. The figure below shows a timeline of the first six months he was responsible for the team. You can see that, slowly but surely, the process helped the team regroup and move into the healthy upper zone. It doesn't happen instantly, but happiness builds steadily and consistently.

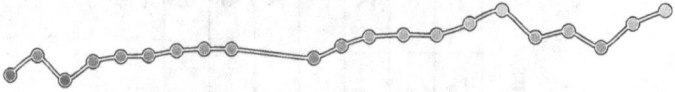

Team happiness building steadily over six months

Turning around a whole organisation

I have been working with one client, ProSearch, for nearly a decade. In 2014 their CEO, Julia Hasenzahl, had a vision. In her words, she 'hit upon the idea that a focus on happiness would help employees thrive in an industry defined by fast-paced technological innovation.'

ProSearch provide eDiscovery services to Fortune 500 corporations and their legal departments. At the time, it was quite a radical idea to start focusing on employee happiness, but in late 2015 I was contacted about working with them. Our first survey was in April 2016, and we still work with them to this day. Here I want to share data on the first two years of their happiness journey. Their quarterly happiness and Five Ways scores are shown in the table below.

Five Ways scores of one client over three years

	Apr-16	Jul-16	Oct-16	Jan-17	Apr-17	Jul-17	Oct-17	Jan-18	Apr-18
Happiness	60	56	66	65	69	73	71	71	76
Connect	69	67	72	73	73	78	78	78	81
Be fair	64	59	66	68	68	74	71	70	78
Empower	62	57	62	63	65	72	70	70	74
Challenge	52	53	55	60	62	69	69	69	72
Inspire	61	64	68	72	71	79	80	78	82

The scores in the table above show the company moving out of the (darker) unhappy and OK zones into the (lighter) happy zone. There was a little blip after the first survey, when they faced some challenges, but over the next two years they persistently and consistently improved their scores across the board.

ProSearch are just one of hundreds of organisations I've worked with over the past decade, and some common patterns have emerged. One thing I've learned is that it's not unusual for scores to dip at the start of the process. Paradoxically, this can be a positive sign – it often means that people are beginning to trust the process, recognise that their feedback is being taken seriously and feel more comfortable sharing honestly. Some organisations also see lower response rates early on, and it's likely that those who don't initially participate are less happy to begin with. As participation improves, average scores may drop – not because things are getting worse, but because the data is becoming more representative.

Meet can be the stumbling block

We've had lots of success stories, but I have to admit there are times when things don't work out. More often than not, the issue isn't with measurement – it's with the meeting. Many organisations struggle to fully commit to this crucial step. There can be a fear that open conversations will unleash a Pandora's box of complaints. In my experience, though, even when scores are poor, honest dialogue often prompts long-overdue change. Measurement surfaces the issues, but only meeting and taking action can resolve them.

Seth Godin, the best-selling author, laments about this lack of attention to the people side of running teams in his recent book on teams (Godin, 2023):

> 'Organisations hire and fire based on vocational skill output all the time, but they practically need an act of the board to get rid of a negative thinker, a bully or a sloth ... If you are wondering why the opportunities you seek aren't materializing, it might be worth looking hard not at the skills that are easy to measure, but at the ones that are important to have.'

People skills are essential skills, especially for leading happy, successful teams. A simple, regular weekly team meeting can help build these skills, while also supporting team performance. When you combine this with measuring team happiness, it becomes easier to spot both strengths and opportunities for improvement, for both teams and their leaders.

Measure-meet-repeat is an excellent habit, and it's the meet element that truly multiplies the impact of happiness on success. As James Clear says, habits are the compound interest of improvement, and this one pays dividends for teams.

Summary

- **We need to measure what matters.** Effective team improvement starts with measurement, but not just any data will do. Using both the (quarterly) Five Ways pulse survey and weekly happiness pulse checks provides a dynamic, real-time picture of how teams are feeling and functioning. Together, these tools highlight where to celebrate and where to improve.

- **It's vital to meet with purpose.** The real magic happens in the meetings. Whether it's a short weekly check-in or a deeper quarterly reflection, these conversations help teams take ownership of their happiness and performance. Actions speak louder than numbers; and meeting regularly turns insight into impact.

- **Repeating the process builds momentum.** Teams thrive not through one-off interventions but through habits. The simple act of measuring, meeting and repeating creates a flywheel of continuous improvement, helping teams become happier, stronger, and more successful over time.

43
Start: Let's Press The Happiness Button

Building happier teams provides a better way of working, and it is aspirational and inspirational. It won't happen by magic, though. New ways of working will need to be adopted for the vision to be put into action. Setting that vision is very much the role of the leader, whether at team or organisational level.

In this book I have put forward many reasons why team happiness matters, including in:

- Stimulating innovation
- Stemming staff turnover
- Avoiding underperformance
- Attracting talent

- Lowering the cost of sales
- Limiting the risk of burnout

Happiness is also seriously good business, as happy teams lead directly to improved results. However, teams and organisations are complex. Each is unique, with its own strengths and challenges, so one size is never going to fit all. One vision isn't, either.

Creating your vision

If you are a leader of one or of many teams, you need to create your own vision, and you need to do it in your own voice. There's no single formula, but most effective visions tend to take one of three broad forms:

- **An inspiring statement.** A short, memorable phrase that captures the spirit of your team or organisation. Think of it as a rallying cry – something people can believe in and repeat. It works best when it connects emotionally and clearly communicates the difference you're trying to make.

- **A set of guiding values.** Rather than setting a destination, this approach focuses on how you want people to behave and make decisions. Values like fairness, creativity or collaboration help shape everyday actions and culture. When clearly defined and consistently applied, values create shared understanding and trust.

- **A vivid description of the future.** This approach paints a picture of what success looks like in practice. It might describe how people will feel, how teams will operate or the kind of impact you'll be having. It's more narrative in style and can help people visualise the journey ahead.

You can, of course, blend these approaches. For example, many organisations combine a core vision statement with a handful of values to clarify how they will get there. What matters most is that your vision feels authentic to you and meaningful to the people you lead.

Choosing your words

I am acutely aware that the word happiness can seem frivolous and un-business–like. The Five Ways can help people understand that team happiness is attractive and energising, that it is about working better together. People can then stop falling into the trap of thinking that happiness is not appropriate at work, or worrying that it means participating in forced fun.

Some leaders feel more comfortable talking about wellbeing than about happiness. I gently encourage them to experiment in dropping the word happiness into their sentences and noticing if people respond differently. Wellbeing can sound corporate and dry, whereas happiness has a lovely, emotional tone to it. I particularly suggest using both – *happiness and wellbeing*. The phrase rolls nicely off the tongue and opens up the emotional power of happiness while maintaining the gravitas of wellbeing.

Language does matter, but your particular context matters even more. For example, digital agencies are very different places to work than distribution warehouses. Management consultancies have entirely different challenges than manufacturing businesses. Your vision needs to be appropriate for your context.

Including yourself and your context

It's also important to include yourself in the vision. You need to create a great culture where teams are happy and success is for everyone, from the newest starter to the oldest hand, from the shop floor to the top floor. Everyone includes you, and being authentic is critical. All of us have different personalities, different strengths and different weaknesses. You being you allows others to be themselves.

Keeping the balance

You need to own the business case, in that you want everyone to enjoy their work but also remember there is work to be done. Great teams are both happy and successful. Feeling good and doing good work go hand in hand – indeed, they build on each other. Building a great culture means everyone wins. If you pretend the drive for happiness is all about the goodness of your heart, people either won't believe you or – even worse – might start to take advantage of your apparent goodwill. It's critical that happiness is placed firmly in the context of work; only then can you unlock all its benefits.

Involving key players

Team leaders are going to play a crucial role, as this is all about building happy and successful teams. In many organisations team leaders are already under a lot of pressure, those two headstrong horses pulling them in different directions. If you lead many teams, then getting their support is going to be critical, and you might want to craft the vision with them. Including them in the process early can only increase the chance of success, even if some are initially unsure.

Once you have set your vision, you need to think about how to put it into action and how to communicate it.

Dealing with resistance and scepticism

It's common to encounter some resistance and scepticism to your new happiness initiative. For some, building happy teams might seem a distraction from 'real work' – the business goals they need to meet. Others might feel burdened with yet another responsibility. *Now I have to look after my team's happiness as well* is a lament I have regularly heard from stressed team leaders. Some might want to embrace the new drive for happiness but have felt let down by organisations before and don't want to run the risk of being disappointed again. A few might be afraid of being exposed as poor people managers, rather than seeing this process as a new learning opportunity.

It's worth remembering that there are always reasons for resistance, and sometimes they are understandable. I always recommend encouraging people to articulate their concerns, to get them out in the open, which might need to be done on a one-to-one basis. It might be that what they really need is more support, especially with regard to time budgets. Some might be suffering from imposter syndrome and need help with their self-confidence. Others might need training on how to adopt a more open coaching approach to their leadership style. Managing teams isn't easy, but with support, team leaders can improve their people skills, which will enhance not only their team's happiness but also their own.

One of the great advantages of measuring team happiness is that there is data to reflect on, discuss and respond to. It brings team happiness more clearly into focus, and the data helps everyone to learn how to work better together.

Press the happiness button – and jam!

Once you have your vision, it is time to share it. Everyone loves to know what is happening, so it is good to lay out the steps in advance. One client I worked with created a fun video to share with everyone, where they playfully outlined:

- **Happiness starts with us.** We want to know how happy we are and, more importantly, how we can be even happier.

- **Pressing the happiness button.** Our first ever 'How happy are we?' survey is live, and we will reveal the results on [date]. When we press the happiness button, every team will be able to see how it is doing.

- **Let's jam!** Next week we will conduct a series of Happiness Jams, which will bring everyone together for fun and focused sessions to share ideas and build action plans.

They captured the essence of the measure-meet-repeat process, and the video was engaging. It helped them get a fantastic response in terms of people answering the survey and participating in the 'jams'. You might well assume this to be some sort of cool tech startup, but in fact the client is a public sector organisation that carries out quality control assessments.

Team happiness can be an inspiring vision, whatever sector you work in. I invite you to press the happiness button and start the process.

Summary

- **You first need to set your vision, your way.** Whether through a bold statement, clear values or a vivid future, your happiness vision needs to feel authentic, meaningful, and right for your context, because one size never fits all.

- **It's important to name the benefits and face the barriers.** Team happiness fuels innovation, retention and performance, but expect some resistance. Taking concerns seriously and offering support helps build trust and momentum.

- **The final step is to press the happiness button ... and jam.** Turning vision into action means inviting people in, building energy and making the first steps engaging. When people see it's serious and uplifting, they're more likely to get on board.

44
Time Restraints: The Biggest Obstacle

Measure-meet-repeat is a simple process, designed to be easy to follow and practical to implement. Let's be honest, though: not everyone is going to embrace it straight away.

Team leaders are under enormous pressure, with many already stretched thin, working long hours and being pulled in multiple directions. It is entirely understandable that some might respond with, *You want me to be responsible for my team's happiness too? I just don't have time for that.*

Of course, we all have the same amount of time – 168 hours a week, to be precise. How we perceive time and how we choose to spend it, though, is a different matter altogether. The issue isn't really about time availability – it's about priorities, and how time is allocated to what really matters. Building team happiness *does* matter. It's not a luxury; it's the foundation for good working relationships, collaboration, trust and sustained success.

Pandora's box

Part of the resistance is a fear of opening Pandora's box – people are afraid they might uncover issues they'd rather not face. It doesn't help that happiness itself feels intangible. It can be difficult to grasp, even we can easily recognise that happiness permeates everything. It's no wonder that addressing happiness can feel out of place in the ordered world of work.

Things are already changing. Increasingly, the conversation in workplaces is shifting from pay and perks to *experience*. Wellbeing, mental health and work–life balance are no longer fringe concerns – they're front and centre, especially for younger generations. Still, many team leaders feel ill-equipped for these discussions and naturally default to avoidance. The problem is that avoidance rarely works. Frustrations don't go away; they just build up.

A simple practice like asking *How was your week? What went well? What didn't?* creates a healthy outlet and establishes a regular rhythm for people to be heard. Over time this builds into a reliable habit – a contained, recurring space where people know they can share openly. *I'll raise that in our weekly check-in* becomes not a burden but a sign of trust and a positive healthy habit.

The power of a contained space

In my therapy training, the concept of a safe, contained space was central – it was the consistency and boundaries of that time that gave the process its power. The same principle applies in teams. A short, weekly meeting – just fifteen to thirty minutes – can offer a dependable, structured space where experiences are shared, challenges are surfaced, and team happiness becomes a normal part of the conversation.

This structured approach aligns with the three Greek gods of time mentioned in Chapter 27:

- **Chronos** – the scheduled time (the meeting itself)
- **Aion** – the repeated rhythm (held every week)
- **Kairos** – the timely moment (where real issues can be addressed)

Regular check-ins serve a dual purpose. They provide a safe space for challenges to be raised and addressed early, preventing issues from festering. Just as important, they create a natural moment to recognise achievements, celebrate progress and appreciate each other's efforts, strengthening relationships and building team happiness along the way.

An investment in time

While I sympathise with team leaders who feel they don't have time to focus on happiness, the truth is that by investing a small amount of time each week, they will save much more time in the long run.

Happy teams are more stable, energetic, collaborative, creative and productive. When leaders neglect team happiness, they risk higher staff turnover, which is one of the most time-consuming and stressful parts of their job.

Happier teams also work more effectively, which means fewer issues escalate up the chain to managers. Problems get solved earlier, decisions get made faster, and the team becomes more self-sufficient.

In the end, investing time in team happiness is not just about their wellbeing. It is also about making the team stronger, more capable and more successful.

Time is limited, but how we use it determines whether we are constantly firefighting or building sustainable success. Team happiness does not require endless meetings or complex initiatives. It requires a small, consistent investment of time and attention. Leaders who embrace this approach will find that time starts working for them, not against them.

Summary

- **Team happiness takes a reasonable amount of time.** A short, weekly check-in can prevent issues from escalating and strengthen team trust and cohesion.

- **Regular space to reflect is powerful.** Scheduled conversations about experience give people a safe outlet to share frustrations and celebrate progress.

- **A small investment pays big dividends.** Happy teams are more resilient, productive, and self-managing, saving leaders time in the long run.

45
How Leaders Can Have Better Conversations

In addition to struggling to make time for happiness check-ins, many team leaders have concerns about how to handle certain conversations. Some feel unprepared for discussions about wellbeing or mental health. This is completely understandable, especially as many managers have had little or no training in essential people skills.

There are of course thousands of books and training courses available on how to be a good team leader, and detailed advice is beyond the scope of this book. However, the whole measure-meet-repeat process is designed precisely so that leaders can learn the necessary skills on the job.

It is still true that the leader's presence and their ability to read the room are important skills that are key to having good conversations that help team members and teams develop. I have found that holding two images in mind can really help. Those images might sound weird to begin with, but stay with me: *mirrors* and *windows*.[45]

Mirrors – listening and reflecting back

A mirror of course reflects back an image so we can see ourselves. In terms of the Five Ways, being a mirror addresses *connect, be fair* and *empower*.

The process of listening and critically reflecting back acts in a similar way. Listening by itself isn't enough – we all need to be listened to and also to know that we have been heard and understood.

This means that just nodding isn't enough. Much better is to paraphrase or summarise what the other person has said. This not only makes them feel heard but also gives them the chance to hear their own words back, which helps clarify things for everyone. If someone gets something not quite right, there is an immediate opportunity for the other person to correct that misunderstanding.

---

45 The idea of using the images of mirrors and windows comes from Appendix A (page 289) of *Imaginization* (Morgan, 1997).

If you are leading a conversation, thinking about how to be a good mirror will help bring the most important points into focus. It also takes the pressure off having to solve everything yourself – the process empowers people to find their own solutions.

Being a good mirror is a great starting point, but it doesn't always go far enough, especially in people leadership roles. This brings me onto windows.

Windows – opening up new possibilities

In contrast to a mirror, a window allows us to look out at the world around us, often from a new perspective. In terms of the Five Ways, being a window leans into the points *challenge* and *inspire*.

Happiness is about good fit – alignment of our inner and outer worlds. A critical part of a team leader's role is aligning their team's inner energy and motivation with the outer goals that need to be achieved. It's important to note, though, that being a good window doesn't mean telling people what to do; it means helping them imagine different ways forward.

Acting as a window and helping the team engage with the broader landscape of the world outside the team is essential.

Whether in team meetings or one-to-ones, remembering to act as both a mirror and a window makes conversations more powerful. Leaders who develop an open, inquiring and supportive style will find their conversations become richer, their teams more engaged and their work not just more successful but also more enjoyable.

Summary

- **Better conversations start with presence.** Many team leaders feel unprepared for people-focused conversations, especially about wellbeing. With measure-meet-repeat they can develop the necessary skills on the job, starting with simply showing up and paying attention.

- **Acting as a mirror improves our listening skills.** Reflective listening helps people feel heard, understood and empowered. Leaders who mirror effectively don't need all the answers – those leaders create clarity and connection by listening and feeding insights back.

- **Being a window offers opportunities.** Great leaders also help people see new possibilities. By opening up perspectives and aligning inner motivation with outer goals, they challenge and inspire their teams towards meaningful progress.

46
When To Flip It Around

I am an advocate for measurement-led approaches and have spent the last decade honing the measure-meet-repeat process. However, it is also possible to flip the process around, starting with actions and then reflecting on how things went, followed by measuring the results. This is especially true with challenges that have no clear way forward. In this chapter I am going to introduce the well-known process called *action learning*, including the hot, tricky issue of flexible working.[46]

Flexible working is a great example of what are often called *wicked problems*.[47] Wicked problems

---

46 There are lots of great resources about action learning on the web. The origin of the process is credited to Reg Ryan (Revans, 1982).
47 The seminal paper in which the concept of wicked problems was first introduced and explored is 'Dilemmas in a general theory of planning' (Rittel and Webber, 1973).

are fiendishly difficult to solve because cause and effect are deeply entwined. Change one thing, and it influences something else in ways you might not expect. Tinkering with flexible working policies is a great example, where you might see benefits in one area but unintended consequences in another. For example, you might empower individuals by allowing remote work, but this can weaken team connection or create fairness issues if there are roles that can't be done remotely.

The key to addressing wicked problems like flexible working isn't to search for a single solution. Instead, it's about creating a process of learning, adapting and evolving as you go. This is where the action-learning approach comes in.

Action learning: The power of experiments

Action learning is a simple but powerful cycle:

- **Plan:** Start with a hypothesis – something you want to test or explore.
- **Act:** Implement a small-scale experiment.
- **Evaluate:** Collect evidence and measure the results.
- **Reflect:** Discuss the findings, learn from them, and adapt your approach.

Then you repeat the cycle, building on what you've learned. Rather than waiting for a perfect plan, you take small steps forward, testing ideas and learning together as a team or organisation.

For tricky challenges like flexible working, an action-learning approach allows you to move forward with curiosity and flexibility. Instead of getting stuck in theoretical debates, you try things out in practice and see what works.

Let's look at some examples around flexible working, to illustrate how experiments can be run.

Experiment 1

- **Plan, action:** Require teams to spend a set number of days together in the office each week.
- **Evaluate:** Did people feel more connected? Did it impact performance, morale, or collaboration?
- **Reflect:** Did team members value the in-person time more than they expected, or did they struggle to make it work?

Experiment 2

- **Plan, action:** Allow teams to set their own hybrid balance.

- **Evaluate:** Review the experiment monthly. How well did this work for individuals, teams, and managers?

- **Reflect:** What tensions arose? What balance felt sustainable?

Each experiment is an opportunity to learn more about what flexible working means in your context. Because every team is different, what works for one might not work for another. By experimenting, you empower teams to find solutions that suit them best.

It is important to take these experiments seriously. They need to be intentional; and evaluating, reflecting and then the next iteration of planning has to happen for them to be more than just a half-hearted attempt.

The most radical experiment?

Possibly the most radical experiment is run by companies that are switching to a four-day working week. This is increasing in popularity, and many organisations try what has become known as the 100-80-100™ model, where all employees in a company pledge to deliver 100% of their work in 80% of the hours and yet still receive 100% of their pay.[48] It is a radical exper-

---

48 The model is the brainchild and trademark of the New Zealand-based entrepreneurs Andrew Barnes and Charlotte Lockhart, who together founded 4DWG, an NGO that promotes the four-day week. See also *Shorter* (Pang, 2020).

iment, but at its core it is just a bold version of the action-learning cycle.

Researchers Professor Juliet Schor from Boston College and Professor Brendan Burchell from Cambridge University tracked more than 120 companies, who all did a six-month trial at the same time (Schor, Burchell et al, 2023). The process involved workshops focusing on how to make organisational productivity gains, as they identified that was where the biggest opportunity was to make immediate 20% increases in efficiency. Over 95% of the companies made the switch permanent after their experiment, which is a very strong endorsement. (It is fair to say, though, that it would be hard for an organisation to roll back on this; a lower-stakes version would be to try this first with a division first.) More impressive was the improvement in employees' mental health and wellbeing. Even indicators showed a significant increase, especially in happiness levels.

It is now more than a century since companies started to switch from six- to five-day weeks, so at a societal level, it could well be time to work shorter hours. However, it is a non-trivial topic, and there are lots of ways of experimenting with shortening working hours without dropping a full day every week. You could experiment, for example, with giving employees the last Friday in each month off, or with nine-day fortnights.

What is for certain is that flexible working and shorter working weeks are both wicked problems that are best approached with an experimental approach. The Five Ways also help focus and deepen these experiments.

No perfect solution

One of the traps organisations fall into is searching for a perfect solution, but wicked problems, by their very nature, don't have perfect solutions. The answers are contextual, depending on the team, the work and the individuals involved. What works now might need to be tweaked later as circumstances change.

The key is to start small. Test ideas, measure what happens, and then adapt. This isn't about getting it right on the first try; it's about learning and improving over time.

Flexible working offers a clear example of this. It can't be solved with a single policy, because it's not a single issue. It touches on empowerment, connection, fairness and growth, all at the same time. By running experiments and learning as you go, you can navigate the complexity without getting stuck.

Learning and moving forward together

The good news is that you don't need to have all the answers when it comes to wicked problems. By taking an action-learning approach, you can empower teams to experiment, reflect and adapt together. Use the Five Ways to Happiness at Work as a guide, and you'll ensure that your experiments are balanced, holistic and aligned with what really matters.

Ultimately, happiness at work isn't about perfection. It's about progress. It's about moving forward together, learning as you go, and creating teams that are both happy and successful, one step at a time.

Summary

- **We need to experiment first, measure second.** For complex, wicked problems like flexible working, it can be better to act first, testing ideas in small, intentional ways; and then reflect and measure the impact before iterating again.

- **Action learning helps us to navigate complexity.** Action-learning cycles – plan, act, evaluate, reflect – offer a practical way to learn your way forward, especially when one-size-fits-all solutions don't exist.

- **Progress beats perfection.** Wicked problems won't be solved overnight, but with a curious mindset and team-led experiments guided by the Five Ways, you can make real, meaningful progress together.

47
A New Focus On Teams

If organisations want to take team happiness seriously, they need to rethink how they support their people – not just as individuals but as teams. Too often, employee wellbeing initiatives focus exclusively on individuals. As highlighted in Chapter 32, wellbeing programmes that focus on individuals generally don't even improve personal wellbeing. Resilience training, mindfulness apps and perks don't have a good return on investment.

In this book I have consistently focused on how the real work happens in teams. This is where great cultures are built, where strong relationships are formed and where success is made.

The problem is that most organisations do not actively measure or manage the team experience. They assume that if individual employees are happy, teams will function well; but this is not how it works in practice. In reality, team dynamics amplify everything: the good, the bad and the ugly. A strong, supportive team makes work more enjoyable, energising and productive. A dysfunctional team, on the other hand, can undermine even the most engaged individuals. Teams are the smallest groups within organisations. They are also the most meaningful and the most impactful.

It is time for a shift from focusing on individual employees to concentrating on teams.

Introducing the head of team experience

To make this shift happen, organisations need to take team experience seriously, and that means supporting team leaders properly.

Many team leaders are under huge pressure at work. They have to manage performance, juggle multiple responsibilities and keep everything running smoothly. On top of that, they are increasingly expected to support their team's wellbeing, without much guidance on how to do it.

Organisations should be asking: *Who is supporting the people who lead our teams?*

This is why there is a need for the role of *head of team experience* – a much better job title than *chief happiness officer* or *head of wellbeing*. Team experience is where happiness and success are both forged, so this new role would get to the heart of both the challenge and the solution.

Whatever you call this role, its focus should be the same: helping leaders create the conditions for team success.

This is not about adding another layer of HR oversight. It is about providing both support and challenge to help leaders:

- Create a culture of trust and collaboration in their teams
- Develop their coaching and listening skills so they can handle challenges effectively
- Balance wellbeing and performance rather than treating them as opposing forces

The best teams do not just happen. They are built; and team leaders need the right support to build them well.

From human resources to resourceful humans (in teams)

This shift is also an opportunity for HR to rethink its role. Many HR professionals got into the field because they care about people, but they too often find themselves stuck in organisational processes, policies and compliance, far removed from the day-to-day experience of looking after people.

By focusing on team experience, HR can step into a new, more meaningful role. Instead of being the enforcer of rules, HR can become the catalyst for great teams, supporting leaders in creating the conditions for happiness and success.

This shift means:

- Helping teams become more self-sustaining, rather than HR fixing problems after they arise

- Giving team leaders practical tools to develop their teams, not just expecting them to figure this out for themselves

- Measuring team culture and dynamics, not just individual engagement scores

Instead of relying too heavily on policies and one-size-fits-all wellbeing initiatives, human resources departments can bring their focus back to where it belongs: creating resourceful humans who love working together in teams.

The big opportunity: Teams as amplifiers

Teams amplify experience. When a team is thriving, the individuals in it thrive. When a team is struggling, individuals feel stuck, disconnected and frustrated.

Organisations spend huge amounts of money on leadership development, engagement surveys and wellbeing initiatives, yet they overlook the biggest amplifier of all: team experience. If organisations want to build workplaces where people enjoy their work, perform at their best and stay committed, they need to move beyond employee experience and focus instead on team experience.

This is not a small tweak. It is a fundamental shift. Employee experience does matter, but teams are where employees' experience is shaped. As highlighted in Chapter 23, data shows that team culture has 2.8 times more impact than organisational culture on employee happiness.

The reality is that happiness at work is not an individual pursuit. It is a collective one. Work happens in teams, success happens in teams, and wellbeing is shaped by team dynamics.

A new focus on team experience would not only benefit employees but also support team leaders and give HR a more purposeful role in shaping workplace culture.

If organisations are serious about making work better, this is one of the first steps to take.

Summary

- **Team experience matters more than individual perks.** While traditional wellbeing programmes focus on individuals, it's the team environment that most strongly shapes people's happiness and performance at work.

- **People who lead teams need to be supported.** Organisations need to properly back team leaders by creating roles like Head of Team Experience, equipping them to foster trust, collaboration and sustainable success.

- **HR can transition from policy enforcer to team enabler.** By focusing on team dynamics, HR can drive meaningful change, supporting resourceful humans working in thriving, high-performing teams.

Conclusion: Happiness Is The Way

Happiness really is a serious business. It's also quietly powerful, boosting team stability, creativity and collaboration in ways we often overlook. Happy teams deliver better service, build stronger client relationships and spark more word-of-mouth recommendations. Suppliers go the extra mile, great candidates are more likely to apply, and even investors benefit. The ripple effects of a happy workplace extend well beyond the office walls.

At its core, happiness is functional – it acts as a signal. When we feel good, it usually means things are working: our relationships are strong, our work feels meaningful, and we're in a supportive environment. When we feel bad, it's often a sign that something needs to change. These signals matter. They help us both steady the ship and know when to shift course.

This dual role – anchoring us and pushing us forward – is especially important in the workplace. Too much focus on change risks burnout. Too much focus on stability leads to stagnation. The real challenge is balance, and happiness helps us strike it.

This book has made the case for why building happy, successful teams isn't a fluffy extra – it's a strategic imperative. That case is grounded in evidence, not wishful thinking.

Part One laid the foundation, showing that happiness isn't just a feeling. It's dynamic, functional and deeply social. It helps us navigate one of the trickiest challenges in working life: balancing the need for stability with the push for change.

Part Two explored how happiness plays out in the work context, both in the day-to-day experience of work and in the culture of our teams. This is where I introduced the Five Ways to Happiness at Work, a practical framework that captures the key drivers of a good working life.

Part Three shared some of my favourite research such as how random variations in weather show, beyond doubt, that happiness drives success. I ended the

CONCLUSION

section by highlighting a powerful finding: happy employees deliver twice the value of those who are just OK, and happier companies grow faster too.

Part Four made the case that the best teams are both happy and high performing. Building those teams takes time, but the Seven Successes of Happy Teams show that it's time well spent. It brings returns not just in output, but in stability, energy and collaboration.

Part Five was a more cautionary section. I looked at the common traps – missteps that individuals, teams and organisations often fall into on the journey to improving wellbeing. These aren't reasons to give up but reminders to intervene thoughtfully.

Part Six brought everything together, focusing on how to put these ideas into practice. It's where the big picture meets day-to-day reality, and where we see just how much influence teams have on both our personal experience of work and wider organisational success.

At the heart of it all is a simple but powerful truth: happiness at work isn't soft or vague – it's dynamic, measurable and deeply tied to team success. When we pay attention to it systematically, happiness becomes more than a nice-to-have. It becomes a driving force for wellbeing, innovation, and, ultimately, success.

New approaches to happiness at work

The Dynamic Model of Team Happiness is at the core of this book. It offers a way to understand how team happiness really works, in all its complexity, with different elements connecting, and influencing each other and, ultimately, shaping performance.

The Five Ways to Happiness at Work provide a practical framework for creating the conditions where happiness can flourish:

1. Connect
2. Be fair
3. Empower
4. Challenge
5. Inspire

Teams are the beating heart of workplace happiness. They're where relationships form, problems get solved and success is shared. A happy team is a successful team, and the great teams are both. The data is clear: happy employees deliver twice as much value as those who are just OK. Unhappy employees, by contrast, often leave before they've even repaid the investment it took to hire them. When teams focus on the Five Ways, happiness grows, and so do the results.

CONCLUSION

The Seven Successes describe what happy teams make possible. They are:

1. Stability

2. Energy

3. Collaboration

4. Creativity

5. Attraction

6. Effectiveness

7. Profit

The power of measurement

Now that you've reached the end of *Happiness Is a Serious Business*, I hope it's clear just how powerful measurement can be for boosting happiness at work. Surveys don't just reflect how people are feeling – they provide clarity, direction and focus. Data is the first step towards meaningful change. It helps teams understand what's working, what's not and where there's room to grow.

Not all measurement is created equal, though. The two survey rhythms below work especially well together, offering complementary insights that help organisations build and sustain happier teams:

- **The quarterly Five Ways pulse survey:** A deeper dive into the drivers of happiness, with actionable insights at both team and organisational levels.

- **The weekly (or monthly) pulse check:** A quicker, light-touch measure that tracks the ebb and flow of team happiness and helps spots any issues early.

Together, these two rhythms create a system that's responsive in the short term but also stays focused on long-term goals – a balance that lies at the heart of lasting success.

Measure-meet-repeat is my practical, measurement-led approach to making happiness part of everyday team life. It's a simple but powerful rhythm:

- **Measure:** Regular weekly pulse checks and occasional deeper surveys generate data that's timely, relevant and actionable.

- **Meet:** Data alone doesn't change anything. What matters is that teams come together to talk about what the results mean. These conversations build awareness, spark ideas and create the motivation to improve how the team works together.

- **Repeat:** Momentum matters. By repeating this process regularly, teams keep happiness and performance front of mind, turning good intentions into ongoing progress.

Sometimes this process can be flipped around. When you're facing complex or wicked problems, the best move is often to try something new first and then measure the impact afterwards.

Whichever way round you begin, the key is rhythm. This repeatable process turns happiness from something abstract into something real – something you can work with, talk about and improve together.

Over to you

The choice is clear: invest in happiness, and you invest in success. Ignore it, and you risk getting stuck in cycles of underperformance, high staff turnover and burnout. The good news? The tools are here, the evidence is strong, and the path forward is clearer than ever.

My aim with this book has been to give you both the confidence and the tools to build happy, successful teams. The specifics will vary – every team is different – but the principles hold. If you follow the approaches I've shared, you'll create the right conditions for happiness and success to take root.

Take what's useful and make it your own. Measure, meet, repeat. Try things out. Reflect, adapt and keep going. That's how you'll build momentum, and the Seven Successes will follow.

Happiness is the way, but there are many ways to happiness. Find the one that fits your team, your culture, your goals. Above all, enjoy the journey – a better world of work starts one team at a time.

Bibliography

Achor, S (2010) *The Happiness Advantage: The seven principles of positive psychology that fuel success and performance at work*, Crown Business

Adams, L (2017) *HR Disrupted: It's time for something different*, Practical Inspiration Publishing

Aked, J, Marks, N, Cordon, C and Thompson, S (2008) 'Five ways to wellbeing: Communicating the evidence', New Economics Foundation, https://neweconomics.org/2008/10/five-ways-to-wellbeing, accessed 28 April 2025

Amabile, TM and Kramer, S (2011) *The Progress Principle: Using small wins to ignite joy, engagement, and creativity at work*, Harvard Business Review Press

Amabile, TM et al (2005) 'Affect and creativity at work', *Administrative Science Quarterly*, 50(3), 367–403, https://doi.org/10.2189/asqu.2005.50.3.367

Ambady, N and Rosenthal, R (1993) 'Half a minute: Predicting teacher evaluations from thin slices of nonverbal behavior and physical attractiveness', *Journal of Personality and Social Psychology*, 64(3), 431–441, https://doi.org/10.1037/0022-3514.64.3.431

Ashcroft et al (2016) *The Relational Lens: Understanding, managing and measuring stakeholder relationships*, Cambridge University Press

Baier, J et al (2023) 'What job seekers wish employers knew', Boston Consultancy Group, www.bcg.com/publications/2023/recruitment-recommendations-for-employers, accessed 29 April 2025

Barrero, JM et al (2025) 'SWAA March 2025 updates', *WFH Research*, https://wfhresearch.com/wp-content/uploads/2025/03/WFHResearch_updates_March2025.pdf, accessed 29 April 2025

Beer, S (1981) *Brain of the Firm (The managerial cybernetics of organization)*, John Wiley & Sons

Bellet, C, de Neve, J-E and Ward, G (2023) 'Does employee happiness have an impact on productivity?', *Management Science*, 69(5), 2599–2617, http://dx.doi.org/10.2139/ssrn.3470734

Bellos, A (2010) *Alex's Adventures in Numberland: Dispatches from the wonderful world of mathematics*, Bloomsbury Publishing PLC

Blanchflower, DG and Oswald, AJ (2019) 'Do humans suffer a psychological low in midlife? Two approaches (with and without controls) in seven data sets', in: M Rojas (ed), *The Economics of Happiness*, Springer, https://doi.org/10.1007/978-3-030-15835-4_19

Bock, L (2015) *Work Rules!: Insights from inside Google that will transform how you live and lead*, Twelve

Bunderson, S and Thompson, JA (2009) 'The call of the wild: Zookeepers, callings, and the double-edged sword of deeply meaningful work', *Administrative Science Quarterly*, 54(1), 32–57, https://doi.org/10.2189/asqu.2009.54.1.32

Bureau of Labor Statistics (2024) 'Employee tenure in 2024', US Department of Labor, www.bls.gov/news.release/pdf/tenure.pdf, accessed 29 April 2025

Camilleri, T, Rockey, S and Dunbar, R (2024) *The Social Brain: The psychology of successful groups*, Penguin

Cappelli, PH (2015) 'Skill gaps, skill shortages, and skill mismatches: Evidence and arguments for the United States', *ILR Review*, 68(2), 251–290, https://doi.org/10.1177/0019793914564961

Chatterjee et al (2020) 'Commuting and wellbeing: A critical overview of the literature with implications for policy and future research', *Transport Reviews*, 40, 5–34, https://doi.org/10.1080/01441647.2019.1649317

Chivers (2024) *Everything Is Predictable: How Bayes' remarkable theorem explains the world*, W&N

Chouinard, Y (2006) *Let My People Go Surfing: The education of a reluctant businessman*, Penguin Group USA

CIPD (no date) 'Organisational climate and culture', Chartered Institute of Personnel and Development, www.cipd.org/uk/knowledge/factsheets/organisation-culture-change-factsheet, accessed 28 April 2025

Clare County Council (2023) 'National award for Clare County Council workplace wellbeing initiatives', Clare County Council, www.clarecoco.ie/your-council/[news]/national-award-for-clare-county-council-workplace-wellbeing-initiatives.html, accessed 3 May 2025

Clark, AE and Oswald, AJ (1994) 'Unhappiness and unemployment', *Economic Journal*, 104(424), 648–659, https://doi.org/10.2307/2234639

Clear, J (2018) *Atomic Habits: An easy and proven way to build good habits and break bad ones*, Random House Business

Cocker, F and Joss, N (2016) 'Compassion fatigue among healthcare, emergency and community service workers: A systematic review', *International Journal of Environmental Research and Public Health*, 13(6), 618, https://doi.org/10.3390/ijerph13060618

Cooperrider, DL and Whitney, D (2005) *Appreciative Inquiry: A positive revolution in change*, Berrett-Koehler Publishers

Covey, SR and Covey, S (2020) *The 7 Habits of Highly Effective People*, Simon & Schuster UK

Csikszentmihalyi, M (1990) *Flow: The psychology of optimal experience*, Harper Perennial

Cummins, A (2019) *The Ultimate Art of War: A step-by-step illustrated guide to Sun Tzu's teachings*, Watkins Publishing

Daisley, B (2022) *Fortitude: The myth of resilience, and the secrets of inner strength*, Cornerstone Press

Damasio, A (2018) *The Strange Order of Things: Life, feeling, and the making of cultures*, Pantheon Books

Darwin, C (1872) *The Expression of the Emotions in Man and Animals*, John Murray

Deci, E and Ryan, R (1980) 'Self-determination theory: When mind mediates behaviour', *The Journal of Mind and Behaviour*, 1 (1), 33–43, www.jstor.org/stable/43852807, accessed 13 June 2025

De Neve, J-E and Ward, G (2025) *Why Workplace Wellbeing Matters: The science behind employee happiness and organizational performance*, Harvard Business Review Press

De Neve, J-E, Kaats, M and Ward, G (2024) 'Workplace wellbeing and firm performance', University of Oxford Wellbeing Research Centre, Working paper 2304, https://doi.org/10.5287/ora-bpkbjayvk

DfE (2023) 'Employer Skills Survey 2022', Department for Education, https://assets.publishing.service.gov.uk/media/672a2743094e4e60c466d160/Employer_Skills_Survey_2022_research_report__Nov_2024_.pdf, accessed 3 May 2025

Dunbar, RIM (1992) 'Neocortex size as a constraint on group size in primates', *Journal of Human Evolution*, 22(6), 469–493, https://doi.org/10.1016/0047-2484(92)90081-J

Dunbar, RIM, Nettle, D and Stiller, J (2003) 'The small world of Shakespeare's plays', *Human Nature*, 14, 397–408, https://doi.org/10.1007/s12110-003-1013-1

Dunbar, RIM (2021) *Friends: Understanding the power of our most important relationships*, Little, Brown

Dyvik, EH (2024) 'Industries with the highest employee burnout rate worldwide in 2019', Statista, www.statista.com/statistics/1274617/industries-burnout-globally, accessed 30 April 2025

Edmans, A (2011) 'Does the stock market fully value intangibles? Employee satisfaction and equity prices', *Journal of Financial Economics*, 101(3), 621–640, https://doi.org/10.1016/j.jfineco.2011.03.021

Edmans, A (2024) *May Contain Lies: How stories, statistics and studies exploit our biases – and what we can do about it*, Penguin

Edmondson, AC (2018) *The Fearless Organization: Creating psychological safety in the workplace for learning, innovation, and growth*, John Wiley & Sons

Eurofound (2019) *Working Conditions and Workers' Health*, Publications Office of the European Union, Luxembourg, www.eurofound.europa.eu/en/publications/2019/working-conditions-and-workers-health, accessed 18 June 2025

Feldman Barrett, L (2017) *How Emotions Are Made: The secret life of the brain*, Macmillan

Fiske, ST, Cuddy, AJ and Glick, P (2007) 'Universal dimensions of social cognition: Warmth and competence', *Trends in Cognitive Sciences*, 11(2), 77–83, https://doi.org/10.1016/j.tics.2006.11.005

BIBLIOGRAPHY

Fleming, W, Ward, G and De Neve, J-E (2024) 'Assessing data quality in a big convenience sample of work wellbeing', University of Oxford Wellbeing Research Centre, https://wellbeing.hmc.ox.ac.uk/wp-content/uploads/2024/06/Assessing-data-quality-March-2024-DOI.pdf, accessed 1 May 2025

Fleming, WJ (2024) 'Employee well-being outcomes from individual-level mental health interventions: Cross-sectional evidence from the United Kingdom', *Industrial Relations Journal*, 55(2), 162–182, https://doi.org/10.1111/irj.12418

Fredrickson, BL (1998) 'What good are positive emotions?' *Review of General Psychology*, 2(3), 300–319, https://https://doi.org/10.1037/1089-2680.2.3.300

Fredrickson, BL (2001) 'The role of positive emotions in positive psychology: The broaden-and-build theory of positive emotions', *American Psychologist*, 56(3), 218–226, https://doi.org/10.1037/0003-066X.56.3.218

Fredrickson, BL (2010) *Positivity: Groundbreaking research to release your inner optimist and thrive*, Simon and Schuster

Fredrickson, BL (2013) *Love 2.0: How our supreme emotion affects everything we feel, think, do, and become*, Hudson Street Press

Fried, DH and Hansson, J (2018) *It Doesn't Have to Be Crazy at Work*, Harper Business

Gallup (2013) 'State of the American workplace: Employee engagement insights for US business leaders', Gallup Workplace, https://workplacebullying.org/multi/pdf/Gallup2013.pdf, assessed 1 June 2025

Gallup (2024) '*State of the Global Workplace: Understanding employees, informing leaders*, Gallup Workplace, www.gallup.com/workplace/349484/state-of-the-global-workplace.aspx, accessed 3 May 2025

Gilbert, P (2009) 'Three types of affect regulation system' [diagram], in Gilbert, P, *The Compassionate Mind: A new approach to life challenges*, Constable and Robinson, diagram 1, p24

Godin, S (2023) *The Song of Significance*, Penguin Business

Grant, A (2014) *Give and Take: Why helping others drives our success*, W&N

Green, F et al (2021) 'Working still harder', *ILR Review*, 75(2), 458–487, https://doi.org/10.1177/0019793920977850

Green, F et al (2024) 'Work and life: The relative importance of job quality for general well-being, and implications for social surveys', *Socio-Economic Review*, 22(2), 835–857, https://doi.org/10.1093/ser/mwae002

Griffiths, J (1999) *Pip Pip: A sideways look at time*, Flamingo

Gueguen, G and Senik, C (2023) 'Adopting telework: The causal impact of working from home on subjective well-being', *British Journal of Industrial Relations*, 61(4), 832–868, https://doi.org/10.1111/bjir.12761

Guest, D and Conway, N (2004) 'Employee well-being and the psychological contract: A report for the CIPD', Chartered Institute of Personnel and Development

Harter, JK et al (2010) 'Causal impact of employee work perceptions on the bottom line of organizations', *Perspectives on Psychological Science*, 5, 378–389, http://dx.doi.org/10.1177/1745691610374589

Helliwell, J et al (2019) *Global Happiness and Wellbeing Policy Report 2019*, Global Happiness Council, https://s3.amazonaws.com/ghwbpr-2019/UAE/GHWPR19.pdf, accessed 29 April 2025

Helliwell, JF et al (2021) *World Happiness Report 2021*, Sustainable Development Solutions Network, https://worldhappiness.report/ed/2021, accessed 25 April 2025

Heskett, JL, Sasser, WE and Schlesinger, LA (1997) *The Service Profit Chain: How leading companies link profit and growth to loyalty, satisfaction, and value*, Free Press

Hewitt, DB et al (2020) 'Evaluating the association of multiple burnout definitions and thresholds with prevalence and outcomes', *JAMA Surgery*, 155(11), 1043–1049, https://doi.org/10.1001/jamasurg.2020.3351

Hsieh, T (2010) *Delivering Happiness: A path to profits, passion and purpose*, Grand Central Publishing

Hughes Johnson, C (2023) *Scaling People: Tactics for management and company building*, Stripe Press

Hunt, T and Pickard, H (2022) 'Harder, better, faster, stronger? Work intensity and "good work" in the UK', *Industrial Relations Journal*, 53(3), 189–206, https://doi.org/10.1111/irj.12364

Hunter, J (2015) 'A bad system will beat a good person every time', The W Edwards Deming Institute, https://deming.org/a-bad-system-will-beat-a-good-person-every-time, accessed 3 May 2025

Indeed Editorial Team (2022) 'Introducing the Indeed Work Happiness Score', Indeed, https://uk.indeed.com/lead/work-happiness-score, accessed 3 May 2025

BIBLIOGRAPHY

Isen, AM, Daubman, KA and Nowicki, GP (1987) 'Positive affect facilitates creative problem solving', *Journal of Personality and Social Psychology*, 52(6), 1122–1131. https://doi.org/10.1037/0022-3514.52.6.1122

Kahn, WA (1990) 'Psychological conditions of personal engagement and disengagement at work', *The Academy of Management Journal*, 33(4), 692–724, www.jstor.org/stable/256287

Kahneman, D et al (2004) 'A survey method for characterizing daily life experience: The day reconstruction method', *Science*, 306(5702),1776–80, https://doi.org/10.1126/science.1103572

Kahneman, D (2012) *Thinking, Fast and Slow*, Penguin

Katzenbach, JR and Smith, DK (1993) *The Wisdom of Teams: Creating the high-performance organization*, Harvard Business School

Laloux, F (2014) *Reinventing Organizations: A guide to creating organizations inspired by the next stage in human consciousness*, Nelson Parker

Lieberman, DZ and Long, ME (2019) *The Molecule of More: How a single chemical in your brain drives love, sex, and creativity – and will determine the fate of the human race*, BenBella Books

Mackey, J and Sisodia, R (2013) *Conscious Capitalism: Liberating the heroic spirit of business*, Harvard Business Review Press

Marks, N (2004) 'The power and potential of well-being indicators: Measuring young people's well-being in Nottingham', New Economics Foundation, www.welldev.org.uk/news/hanse-pdfs/nottingham-pdf1.pdf, accessed 29 April 2025

Marks, N and Thompson, S (2008) 'Measuring well-being in policy: Issues and applications', New Economics Foundation, https://neweconomics.org/2008/10/measuring-wellbeing-policy

Maslow, A (1943) 'A theory of human motivation', *Psychological Review*, 50, 370–396, https://doi.org/10.1037/h0054346

McIntosh, (2013) 'Hollowing out and the future of the labour market', Department for Business Innovation and Skills, https://assets.publishing.service.gov.uk/media/5a7c286ce5274a1f5cc76281/bis-13-1213-hollowing-out-and-future-of-the-labour-market.pdf, accessed 3 May 2025

Melnick, ER et al (2020) 'The association between perceived electronic health record usability and professional burnout among US physicians', *Mayo Clinic Proceedings*, 95(3), 476–487, https://doi.org/10.1016/j.mayocp.2019.09.024

Morgan, G (1986) *Images of Organization*, SAGE Publications

Morgan, G (1997) *Imaginization: New mindsets for seeing, organizing, and managing*, SAGE Publications

Office for National Statistics (2024) 'Labour Force Survey' [data series], 11th Release, UK Data Service, SN: 2000026, http://doi.org/10.5255/UKDA-Series-2000026

Pang, AS-K (2020) *Shorter: How smart companies work less, embrace flexibility and boost productivity*, Penguin Business

Penn Arts & Sciences (no date) 'Penn Resilience Program and PERMA™ Workshops', University of Pennsylvania Positive Psychology Center, https://ppc.sas.upenn.edu/services/penn-resilience-training, accessed 3 May 2025

Pink, D (2011) *Drive: The surprising truth about what motivates us*, Canongate Books

Pixar (2015) *Inside Out*, Pixar Animation Studios

Prilleltensky, I (2012) Wellness as fairness', *American Journal of Community Psychology*, 49, 1–21, http://dx.doi.org/10.1007/s10464-011-9448-8

Quoidbach, J et al (2019) 'Happiness and social behavior', *Psychological Science*, 30(8), 1111–1122, https://doi.org/10.1177/0956797619849666

Reichheld, FF (2001) *Loyalty Rules! How today's leaders build lasting relationships*, Harvard Business School Press

Revans, RW (1982) 'What is action learning?', *Journal of Management Development*, 1(3), 64–75, https://doi.org/10.1108/eb051529

Rittel, HWJ and Webber, MM (1973) 'Dilemmas in a general theory of planning', *Policy Sciences*, 4, 155–169, https://doi.org/10.1007/BF01405730

Samiri, I and Millard, S (2022) 'Why is UK productivity low and how can it improve?', National Institute of Economic and Social Research, https://niesr.ac.uk/blog/why-uk-productivity-low-and-how-can-it-improve, accessed 30 April 2025

Schaninger, B, Hancock, B and Field, E (2023) *Power to the Middle: Why managers hold the keys to the future of work*, Harvard Business Review Press

Schor, J, Burchell, B et al (2023) 'The results are in: The UK's four-day week pilot', 4 Day Week Global, https://salford-repository.worktribe.com/preview/1502677/The-results-are-in-The-UKs-four-day-week-pilot.pdf, accessed 5 May 2025

Scott, K (2017) *Radical Candor: Be a kick-ass boss without losing your humanity*, St Martin's Press

Seel, NM (2012) 'Duncker, Karl (1903–1940)', *Encyclopedia of the Sciences of Learning*, Springer, https://doi.org/10.1007/978-1-4419-1428-6_1936

Seligman, ME (2011) *Flourish: A visionary new understanding of happiness and well-being*, Simon and Schuster

Senge, PM (2006) *The Fifth Discipline: The art and practice of the learning organization*, Random House Business

Seth, A (2021) *Being You: A new science of consciousness*, Faber & Faber

Sinek, S (2011) *Start with Why: How great leaders inspire everyone to take action*, Penguin

Tennant, R et al (2007) 'The Warwick-Edinburgh Mental Wellbeing Scale (WEMWBS): Development and UK validation', *Health and Quality of Life Outcomes*, 5(63), https://doi.org/10.1186/1477-7525-5-63

Trusov, M, Bucklin, RE and Pauwels, KH (2009) 'Effects of word-of-mouth versus traditional marketing: Findings from an internet social networking site', *Journal of Marketing*, 73(5), 90–102, https://dx.doi.org/10.2139/ssrn.1129351

TUC (2023) 'UK workers put in £26 billion worth of unpaid overtime during the last year – TUC analysis', TUC, www.tuc.org.uk/news/uk-workers-put-ps26-billion-worth-unpaid-overtime-during-last-year-tuc-analysis, accessed 2 May 2025

VA (2022) *2022 National Veteran Suicide Prevention Annual Report*, US Department of Veterans Affairs, www.mentalhealth.va.gov/docs/data-sheets/2022/2022-National-Veteran-Suicide-Prevention-Annual-Report-FINAL-508.pdf, accessed 3 May 2025

Vermeylen, G et al (2012) '5th European Working Conditions Survey – overview report', Eurofound, www.eurofound.europa.eu/en/publications/2012/fifth-european-working-conditions-survey-overview-report

Vittersø, J (2025) *Humanistic Wellbeing: Toward a value-based science of the good life*, Springer

Volmer, J (2012) 'Catching leaders' mood: Contagion effects in teams', *Administrative Sciences*, 2(3), 203–220, https://doi.org/10.3390/admsci2030203

Ward, G (2023) 'Workplace happiness and employee recruitment', *Academy of Management Proceedings*, 2023(1), https://doi.org/10.5465/AMPROC.2023.132bp

Warr, P (2011) *Work, Happiness, and Unhappiness*, Psychology Press

Whitman, DS et al (2010) 'Satisfaction, citizenship behaviors, and performance in work units: A meta-analysis of collective construct relations', *Personnel Psychology*, 63, https://doi.org/10.1111/j.1744-6570.2009.01162.x

WHO (2019) 'Burn-out an "occupational phenomenon": International classification of diseases', World Health Organization, www.who.int/news/item/28-05-2019-burn-out-an-occupational-phenomenon-international-classification-of-diseases, accessed 30 April 2025

Whyte, D (2011) *The House of Belonging*, Many Rivers Press

Wolter, JS et al (2019) 'Employee satisfaction trajectories and their effect on customer satisfaction and repatronage intentions', *Journal of the Academy of Marketing Science* 47(3), 815–836, https://doi.org/10.1007/s11747-019-00655-9

Yang, M (2022) 'Meta employees left to do their own laundry as perks get cut', *The Guardian*, www.theguardian.com/technology/2022/mar/11/meta-employees-perks-cut-free-laundry

Acknowledgements

Writing a book is not a solo pursuit. It's not an easy one either! I have struggled a lot at times. I knew it was going to be a painful process, and at the beginning I tried working with a writer, Ivor Lee. His patience and support really got me started, though it ultimately showed me that I needed to find my own voice. I'd also like to thank Euan Thorneycroft from the AM Heath Literary Agency. He encouraged me to write a book, and although we didn't end up bringing it to publication together, he certainly supported me and challenged me to become a better writer.

My biggest support during the process was my coach, the wonderful Dominique Fayolle. She got me writing every day, and over time my sentences started to flow better. It was quite a process for a statistician who, although a good speaker, had never been a confident writer. For any budding writers, I would recommend a coach, or a perhaps a peer-support group; writing is a lonely process, and support is critical.

I have worked with many people over the last few decades, who have shaped my work and thinking. Initial sparks came from Manfred Max-Neef, Nan Beecher Moore and Charles Handy, who were all personally supportive. Many others, such as Stafford Beer, Antonio Damasio, Robin Dunbar and Gareth Morgan, I have met only through their books.

When I started out exploring happiness and wellbeing in public policy, I received so much advice and wisdom from experts in the field: Teresa Amabile, Ed Diener, Barbara Fredrickson, John Helliwell, Chris Peterson and Ruut Veenhoven, to mention just a few.

The team I built at the New Economics Foundation shaped me as much as – if not more than – I shaped them. I'm especially grateful to Saamah Abdallah, Jody Aked, Juliet Michaelson, Nicola Steuer and Sam Thompson. Saamah and Jody continued to collaborate with me on happiness at work for many years afterward.

Since 2012 I have worked with my patient business partner Rich Aston. He built all the tech behind the Friday Pulse platform and helped design the models and algorithms that sit behind it. Angela Miles has looked after our clients over the years, and her attention to detail has made me face contradictions and any lack of consistency in my writing. Ian Townsend helped with early modelling of the employee lifetime value metric, and Parul Singh with developing the personal happiness test.

Several people have read and commented on drafts, many of which are long since abandoned. Thank you to Kenneth Boughton, Rawdie Marks, Joanna McCulloch, Mary Murphy, Maggi Rose, Rich Russakoff and Sarah Tomley. Both my sister Caroline Marks and my mother Angela Marks lent me their houses when they were away so I could have a quiet retreat to write in. That certainly helped me focus.

The team at Rethink Press have been really supportive in the publication process, especially Joe Gregory, Ilsa Hawtin and Kathy Steeden.

My wife Zoe has been especially patient and has cheered me up when I've needed a happiness boost. I hope to return the support to her in the future.

The Author

Nic Marks is a pioneering figure in the field of workplace wellbeing, often described as The Happiness Statistician for his unique combination of analytical insight and human understanding. Originally trained as a mathematician and statistician, Nic has spent the past 25 years at the forefront of measuring what matters – people's experience of life and work.

After graduating from Cambridge, he studied operational research and organisational change, while also training as a therapist – an unusual mix that has come to define his work. Nic founded the Centre for Wellbeing at the New Economics Foundation (NEF), where he and his team developed influential frameworks such as the Happy Planet Index and the Five Ways to Wellbeing. His TED talk on happiness has been viewed millions of times, and he was the author of one of the first TEDbooks, *A Happiness Manifesto*.

In 2012, Nic founded Friday Pulse, a London-based tech company helping organisations measure and improve team happiness through a science-led weekly pulse. His clients include large corporates, public sector organisations and fast-growth scale-ups – teams of every shape and size.

Nic's work sits at the intersection of statistics, psychology and systems thinking. He brings evidence, empathy and optimism to his mission: to make happiness at work something we take seriously. He's an engaging public speaker, whether at boardroom briefings, international summits or music festivals.

Nic lives near Stonehenge in Wiltshire with his wife. He's happiest when walking the ancient chalk paths of southern England, listening to music, or enjoying time with his family, as well as occasionally getting immersed in datasets.

- nicmarks.org
- www.linkedin.com/in/marksnic

THE AUTHOR

About Friday Pulse

Friday Pulse helps organisations understand, track and build team happiness. Their science-led platform gives teams a voice and leaders the insights they need to create happier, more successful workplaces. Based on years of wellbeing research and practical experience, Friday Pulse measures key drivers of team happiness; provides real-time data; and supports regular, meaningful conversations. By combining weekly pulse checks with quarterly deep dives, the platform creates a rhythm of feedback, reflection and improvement. Trusted by companies around the world, Friday Pulse turns wellbeing from a vague ideal into a clear, actionable priority, because happiness at work is a serious business.

🌐 https://fridaypulse.com

www.ingramcontent.com/pod-product-compliance
Lightning Source LLC
Chambersburg PA
CBHW010926180426
43192CB00043B/2781